Remembering
COLUMBIA
South Carolina

To Robert, a fellow
historian & good author
May you enjoy this
"walk through Columbia"
in good health &
spirits

All the best,
Miles S. Richards
6 October 2007

Remembering
COLUMBIA
South Carolina

Capital City Chronicles

DR. MILES S. RICHARDS

Charleston   London

History
PRESS

Published by The History Press
Charleston, SC 29403
www.historypress.net

Cover Image: View of Main Street in Columbia, circa 1920s. *Historic Columbia Foundation*

First published 2006

Manufactured in the United Kingdom

ISBN 1.59629.112.5

Library of Congress Cataloging-in-Publication Data

Richards, Miles.
 Remembering Columbia, South Carolina : capital city chronicles / Miles Richards.
 p. cm.
 ISBN 1-59629-112-5 (alk. paper)
 1. Columbia (S.C.)--History--20th century--Anecdotes. 2. Columbia
(S.C.)--Biography--Anecdotes. 3. Columbia (S.C.)--Social life and
customs--20th century--Anecdotes. I. Title.
 F279.C7R53 2006
 975.7'71--dc22
 2006012655

Notice: The information in this book is true and complete to the best of our knowledge. It is offered without guarantee on the part of the author or The History Press. The author and The History Press disclaim all liability in connection with the use of this book.

Contents

Introduction

Throughout the last decade I have had occasion to peruse regularly issues of the respective major South Carolina newspapers that were published in the first decades of the twentieth century. Many of these journals are preserved upon microfilm within the collection of the South Caroliniana Library at the University of South Carolina. While undertaking several major research projects, I found the Columbia *Record* to be especially informative. Numerous local events, described in rich detail, were to be found in virtually every issue. The editors apparently made a conscious effort to include stories calculated to be of interest to their readership. Consequently, I frequently paused in my main research to write down the details of these interesting vignettes. Most of these stories have not been included within the monographs dealing with either Columbia or Richland County. I realized that this material was portraying a Columbia that is a "dead world" to most local city residents. And I also perceived that many of these persons actually were interested in knowing about this forgotten past.

By 1997, I had published an article on Paul R. Redfern, the noted Columbia aviator of the 1920s, within *Carologue*, the South Carolina Historical Society's popular magazine. Several of my other features subsequently appeared in newspapers around the state. In the process, I began to specialize in writing about those events that had happened during the first half of the last century. Initially, many of these essays were culled from within my existing research notes. But I also began to read regularly the myriad of *Record* issues on microfilm. Most of the stories in this book were gained in this manner. Assorted South Caroliniana staff employees have been watching this endeavor progress over the years and they have encouraged me to publish a collection of these vignettes. The majority of these tales have not appeared in print since they originally ran in the *Record*. Furthermore, all of these essays factually recount actual events.

For this monograph I have selected episodes that occurred around Columbia as well as Richland and Lexington Counties from 1900 until 1935. These works collectively present a city that has changed considerably in physical appearance during the past century. For instance, the various main city thoroughfares possessed trolley tracks and were unpaved. Despite the advent of the automobile, numerous horse-drawn vehicles still were to be seen moving about on these streets. Upon much of the acreage approaching the Congaree River stood textile mills, warehouses and railroad facilities. And viable residential neighborhoods were located throughout the downtown, within easy walking distance of the main business district. Significantly, many of those homeowners continued to utilize barns, chicken coops and cisterns situated upon their properties. The initial planned suburban subdivisions, notably Shandon and Wales Garden, were only beginning to develop. Not surprisingly, lying beyond the city limits was endless rural countryside. Within several stories, moreover, are mentioned prominent downtown landmarks, such as the Columbia Opera House and the Jefferson Hotel, which were demolished in later decades.

Upon perusing these vignettes readers will discern that human behavior has not changed perceptibly during the past century. For instance, all too frequently city residents were prone to violence. Many Columbians habitually carried firearms and knives, which they did not hesitate to use. Many personal disputes were settled either by gunfire or sharp knife thrusts. Violent crimes often were connected to the widespread bootlegging activities occurring around town. Although South Carolina officially was a "dry state," even before Prohibition, countless local residents actively participated in the illicit liquor trade. And they were prepared to risk possible legal prosecution.

A notable aspect of many stories is the complex nature of race relations in Columbia during that period. While segregation was established firmly, southerners of both races were obliged to remain in intimate daily social contact. But black South Carolinians clearly were forced to assume subservient roles. Within most of these stories African Americans were usually performing either unskilled manual labor or domestic work for demanding white employers. The *Record* also consistently maintained the prevailing practice of making sure that readers knew when a person was African American. Next to the name invariably was to be found the designations "colored" and "negro." They always placed both words in the lowercase. Furthermore, race etiquette precluded that African Americans ever were referred to as "Mr." or "Mrs." and any professional designations routinely were ignored by the white reporters. These journalistic practices may be discerned amidst many direct quotations throughout the book.

Meanwhile, many essays demonstrate that black Columbians frequently were the persons routinely being subjected to criminal punishment, usually stints upon chain gangs. Within the South Carolina judicial system they invariably were considered "guilty until proven innocent." Their white counterparts, however, often received lenient treatment within those same courts. A common practice was for white murderers to be prosecuted on the lesser charge of manslaughter, but black offenders seldom gained similar arrangements. The former group frequently gained parole within a few years, while the latter faced execution. Certain African Americans periodically did manage to obtain "maneuvering room" within the southern criminal justice as well as other aspects of the "Jim Crow" system. As this book demonstrates, though, such occurrences were not commonplace.

During recent years the author has noted that many persons are beginning to reside again within the city, including the downtown. A concerted effort is being made locally to revive Columbia's primary business district. Various notable city buildings, dating from the early twentieth century, are being accorded considerable "adaptive reuse" by both preservationists and developers. Accordingly, these new city residents should learn something about the city's past and those persons complaining about current "urban ills" should realize that the same problems were prevalent at the commencement of the previous century. In essence, though, this book is meant to reacquaint readers with many long-forgotten historical episodes in Columbia that deserve to be remembered.

Part I

Flying on the Fourth of July at Night

On July 4, 1923, Paul R. Redfern, Columbia's noted young aviator, was planning to celebrate the holiday in a noteworthy manner. He intended to undertake the first known aerial voyage at night over the city. Apparently, no South Carolina pilot previously had attempted to take off after sundown. And he invited a Columbia *Record* reporter, John B. Crews, to be his passenger on this occasion. Crews already had flown with him on two earlier daylight sojourns.

About 10:30 p.m., the pilot's monoplane lifted off from an air strip at the State Fair Grounds on the Assembly Street extension. Only a handful of onlookers, including Redfern's usual mechanic, Daniel Berkman, had witnessed the departure. In seeking to avoid dealing with a crowd of meddlesome spectators, he had not publicized this project. Once airborne, as well as reaching eight hundred feet in altitude, the aircraft began to circle over the southern end of the city for thirty minutes.

Not surprisingly, neither Redfern nor Crews could discern the usual landmarks on the ground. Consequently, his father, Dr. Frederick C. Redfern, drove a Packard roadster, with two oil lanterns tied to the back of the vehicle. In essence, the aviator attempted to follow his father's route along the various roadways. Furthermore, the noise of the engine overhead quickly had attracted the attention of numerous Columbians. And to celebrate the holiday both fliers periodically dropped lighted firecrackers, along with leaflets explaining the mission. By the time the plane was approaching the landing strip, various motorists had formed a cavalcade behind Dr. Redfern's automobile.

Meanwhile, Berkman and several helpers had erected a large bonfire next to the airstrip. As Crews later wrote, "The signal lights burned welcomingly as the airship turned its nose again toward the landing field." At this point, a large crowd was on hand to welcome the sojourners from their brief adventure. Another journalist noted, "To the accompaniment of the whirling propeller, the graceful craft landed again on terra firma."

During an impromptu news conference Redfern declared that several other night flights already were in the planning stage "for the near future." But these subsequent "aerial voyages" would be advertised heavily in advance. On these flights, he planned to "place red lanterns on the tail of the plane and those persons interested…will be able to follow the course of the aircraft through space." Redfern was pleased to accomplish this local aerial milestone upon the Fourth of July. Aerial night flight within South Carolina now was an established fact.

Once his aerial reputation was established, Redfern began to take passengers on day trips around the state. Later he started to make flights to other states throughout the Southeast. By 1924, he spent the summer months in Dayton, Ohio; in the winter, he made his base of operations in Columbia. During his spare time Redfern gave public "stunt" exhibitions that demonstrated his flying skills.

With the backing of several wealthy investors, in August 1927, Redfern attempted to fly a monoplane nonstop from Brunswick, Georgia, to Rio de Janeiro, a sojourn of 4,700 miles. Although he was observed later over the interior of Venezuela, the pilot never reached his destination. For many years there continued to be widespread international interest in Redfern's fate. By September 16, 1927, his relatives had offered a $1,000 reward to anyone who found him, alive or dead. To date, though, no tangible traces of either Redfern or his airplane have ever been found.

But it should not be forgotten that Redfern did complete the first solo flight over the Caribbean Sea. He also managed to make the initial direct flight between North and South America. All of that, however, lay far in the future during that Fourth of July night in 1923.

They Wanted to View Some Stunts

By June 1928, the exploits of various aeronauts, including Paul R. Redfern, were causing considerable public interest in aviation. Accordingly, many Columbia residents were delighted when William T. Huffman announced that a stunt pilot, Donald "Dusty" Bunnard, would be performing a flying exhibition at Twin Lakes Resort on June 18. Huffman's popular "swimming hole" was situated off Garner's Ferry Road, approximately six miles east of the city. Various publicity leaflets announced that Bunnard was planning "an impressive array of aerial stunts " for the general public.

The pilot had flown his monoplane in from Greensboro, North Carolina, on June 12. Initially, he had placed his machine within a hangar at the State Fair Grounds and Huffman had made a reservation for him at the Jefferson Hotel on Main Street. Various observers agreed that the mild-mannered Bunnard did not conform to the swaggering, hard-drinking image invariably associated with barnstorming aviators. For instance, no one spotted him carousing around the downtown during his visit. But numerous eyewitnesses observed Bunnard flying his aircraft over the city.

Consequently, a large assemblage had gathered at Twin Lakes to observe the exhibition. Early that morning the pilot had flown his plane out to the resort. The monoplane was sitting in a barn adjacent to an airstrip, recently created within an old cornfield. Around 2:00 p.m., Bunnard was seen climbing into his open cockpit. The onlookers, though, were unaware that he was ambivalent about his upcoming flight. He had been complaining to a helper that the high winds circulating around the field would be a definite problem. The aviator also groused that the overflow crowd was "constantly getting in his way." Nevertheless, he needed the $150 that Huffman was paying him for the stunts.

While heading down the runway Bunnard was horrified that various clusters of spectators were standing directly in his path. Upon swerving to miss them, Bunnard found that now he was heading toward a parked tractor. Because he was forced to make a premature takeoff, the plane went airborne at a sharp angle and the strong wind gusts precluded any attempts at aerial acrobatics. After circling the field three times Bunnard made a relatively solid landing. Unfortunately, however, his problems were just beginning. While awaiting the exhibition many of the onlookers had been imbibing corn liquor.

Apparently, a local bootlegger that afternoon was enjoying a "thriving business" within a nearby patch of woods. Numerous drunken spectators were incensed that Bunnard had not completed his demonstration. A University of South Carolina geology professor, Julian J. Petty, disgustedly recalled that many onlookers "began acting like a lynch mob." Although several rowdies expressed a desire to inflict a physical beating upon the pilot, he had already fled the scene. Instead, they converged upon the airplane for the purpose of procuring some souvenirs.

They commenced to rip off much of the fabric covering the aircraft. Meanwhile, other hooligans lit matches and "reduced the machine to a seething mass of embers." As the Columbia *Record* declared, "Many of these folk evidently wanted to see exactly how a plane burns." Not surprisingly, the flames also ruined the engine beyond repair. An incredulous Bunnard had watched all of this wanton destruction from the upper floor of the resort's main building. Interestingly, no sheriff deputies reached Twin Lakes until an hour after the trouble.

After most spectators had departed, the disconsolate pilot walked over to view the wreckage. He sorrowfully told several companions that his monoplane was "a total loss, worthless even to salvagers." At Huffman's request, Professor Petty subsequently drove the flier back to Columbia, where he wasted little time checking out of the Jefferson. In any case, Bunnard's employer readily paid him $200 in cash for his horrific experience. By 7:00 p.m., the pilot was aboard an Atlantic Coast Line train, bound for Salisbury, North Carolina. Before boarding, Bunnard vigorously assured the professor that he never planned any return visit to Columbia "in this lifetime."

A Most Noisy Main Street Fire

During the evening of August 17, 1913, the majority of guests at the Columbia Hotel were in bed by midnight. Within several hours, though, they were awakened suddenly when the hotel's fire bell began ringing. After emerging from their rooms they were told that the rear section of the building was on fire. They also heard that much of the 1500 block of Main Street was "up in flames."

About 4:00 a.m., the fire had begun within the second floor of the Lorick & Laurence Mercantile Store at 1525 Main Street. That business specialized in quality dry goods and much of the inventory was stored upon the upper floors. A fire investigator later determined that the blaze was ignited by a dust explosion, which eventually consumed the entire building. The Columbia *Record* declared, "The firemen had to fight the flames within a narrow alley and the blaze proved to be a very stubborn one." Their problems were compounded "at frequent intervals" by unforeseen violent explosions, because Lorick & Laurence had considerable amounts of bullets and gunpowder in stock. "These bright explosions certainly added a spectacular scene to the occasion," a reporter added. A thoroughly disconsolate Preston C. Lorick admitted to several onlookers that his business was "a total loss."

In any case, the flames spread quickly to the Columbia Hotel's rear kitchen. An alert African American porter, Moses Deas, however, began sounding the fire bell that stood outdoors in the back alley. The guests obviously were frightened by the explosions and "the nearness of the flames." Accordingly, they fled through

16

the front door "without waiting to robe themselves in their day garments." But several women expressed great personal chagrin about standing in their night garments on Main Street. A Southern Railways employee, Anson Jones, unwisely had decided to jump from his second story window. He was lucky to escape only with a broken ankle. Due to the steady, efficient work of the manager, Samuel F. Wheeler, and his employees, no other patron sustained a major injury.

Meanwhile, the Columbia Hotel's rear section experienced severe structural damage. "Most of the hotel furnishings were either burned or damaged by smoke and water," the *Record* noted. And many of the guests had lost their luggage to the blaze. The majority of the displaced patrons were provided temporary lodging at various other downtown hostelries and boarding houses. The police reported that an enterprising pickpocket, Willie "Black Boy" Pitts, had lifted the wallets of several spectators amidst all of the commotion. Upon being "caught in the act" by Police Sergeant Perry W. Knox, this slick con artist wound up in the Columbia City Jail.

About 6:00 a.m., the entire south wall of the Lorick & Laurence collapsed, nearly burying six firemen beneath the fiery embers. Fire Chief William J. May told reporters that several of his men had been overcome by the thick smoke. But they revived quickly upon being transported to Columbia Hospital for medical treatment. Various firemen also received minor burns from "flaming debris." Their wounds were treated with ointments supplied by Wingfield's Drug Store. A relieved Chief May later declared, "All told, we almost got out of this thing unscathed." Following the "strenuous work" by the firefighters the blaze finally was extinguished around noon.

Along with the hotel several other businesses adjacent to Lorick & Laurence received severe fire damage. The Jones Crockery Company and Weinberg's Carpet Store were "totally destroyed" by the flames. The respective merchants collectively lost about $250,000. Not surprisingly, only a fraction of those costs were covered by fire insurance. A journalist observed, "Collateral water and smoke damage may be added to the fire loss."

Throughout the next two days a contingent of firemen kept a "constant vigil" over the smoldering ruins. Countless pedestrians paused to stare at this grim sight as well. Everyone agreed that this was among the worst fires seen in downtown Columbia since the Civil War.

Lightning Struck Twice One Day

On August 25, 1925, about 4:00 p.m., a violent thunderstorm was passing through southern Richland County. Not surprisingly, lightning frequently streaked across the sky, greatly worrying numerous spectators upon the ground. Incredibly, in separate accidents two unlucky travelers were killed by lightning bolts within the vicinity of Hopkins.

While making his rounds on horseback, Edward House, a forty-five year old African American mail carrier, was riding down a rural lane. Consequently, he sought shelter underneath a nearby large oak tree. While waiting out the deluge, lightning suddenly scored a direct hit upon the unfortunate man. Apparently, he was killed "instantly," while the bolt shattered the tree as well. But House's horse escaped the accident unscathed. Several farm workers later discovered the mount trotting down the road toward Hopkins. As may be expected, most of the tree limbs had fallen directly across the roadway. As workmen were clearing away this debris they found House's corpse. Coroner J. Blakely Scott of Richland County reached the accident scene two hours later. He quickly determined that the mail carrier had died "by electrocution from the lightning." He probably was dead already when several large limbs landed upon his body. Meanwhile, Coroner Scott had learned that another fatal accident had occurred approximately two miles away.

Prior to the storm a black sharecropper, twenty-three year old John Edmunds, was driving a buggy down another country roadway. Desperate to reach his cabin, he deliberately refused to stop for a neighbor, Mrs. Kate Bracy, who was walking in the same direction. Quite unwittingly, though, Edmonds actually saved Bracy's life. Several minutes later the buggy driver was fatally struck by a powerful lightning bolt. As the Columbia *Record* noted, "The mule which was hitched to the vehicle was killed and the buggy was totally burned." After waiting out the storm in a vacant shack, Mrs. Bracy came upon the grisly scene. She noticed that the victim's body was "burnt almost beyond recognition." She quickly reached a nearby farmer's house and telephoned Deputy Sheriff Benjamin T. Rice, a Hopkins resident.

In any case, Coroner Scott and various other observers could not recall any other occasion when two fatal lightning accidents had happened within such close proximity. These tragedies certainly underscored the inherent danger in being outside during a violent thunderstorm. Apparently, Edmund's selfish behavior had received its "just reward." These deaths also proved that nearby to Hopkins one fateful afternoon lightning certainly had struck twice, with most deadly results.

Out With the Garbage

About 4:00 p.m., on July 7, 1924, Walter Griffin, an African American employee of the South Carolina Penitentiary, drove a pickup truck out of the prison grounds. Three times a week he transported a load of refuse to a garbage dump, situated nearby to Elmwood Cemetery. During these cross-town sojourns he was usually accompanied by a helper, Lafayette Du Bose. But some hidden passengers also went along for the ride. Two white convicts, John Driggers and Ben Long, were concealed within the smelly rubbish. And Griffin was well aware of their presence.

By all accounts, the two escapees were "pretty wily operators." Driggers was serving ten years for a highway robbery in Spartanburg County. Meanwhile, Long was spending eight years for a series of burglaries around Columbia. The latter convict also was known to be among the best safecrackers in the Carolinas. Furthermore, they already had been involved in two botched escape attempts. Inexplicably, though, Superintendent A. Malcolm Scarborough had failed to place either man under close supervision. Apparently, Driggers had paid ten dollars to Griffin for his assistance. And another five dollars later was promised to Du Bose.

Accordingly, the two convicts met the truck within the loading dock behind the prison kitchen. Without the slightest hesitation, the would-be escapees descended into the smelly refuse. Both men remained hidden while the truck exited the main gate and traversed through downtown Columbia. Upon reaching the dump beyond Elmwood Street, the two inmates took their leave. The two African Americans last observed the two men walking briskly through Elmwood Cemetery. Griffin suspected that they were heading toward a rendezvous with some confederate. Several hours later police investigators discovered their prison uniforms hidden under some bushes next to Southern Railway tracks. Most commentators believed that they had clambered aboard a passing freight train.

In any case, their successful escape was discovered during the evening roll call. An informant subsequently told Superintendent Scarborough about their bizarre escape method. The next morning Griffin and Du Bose were taken into custody. They ultimately were sentenced to two years upon the state chain gang. Of course, their cash payments were confiscated by irate penitentiary officials.

Three weeks later Long was apprehended in Cheraw, South Carolina, where he was staying with an intimate woman companion. Nearly four months passed, however, before Driggers was arrested out in Harlem, Georgia. He had been captured following an abortive bank robbery. Both fugitives were transported back to Columbia to serve out their sentences.

Both convicts readily admitted that their escape ride had been singularly unpleasant. But they were intent upon gaining their freedom at any cost. Veteran commentators could not recall any similar breakout attempts. Accordingly, Scarborough assured reporters that all subsequent garbage hauls would be closely inspected by vigilant guards.

The Wrong Guilty Man

On July 14, 1924, Chief of Police Fred S. Strickland received a wire from Columbus, Ohio, which provoked "several days of mystery" for the Columbia police force. His counterpart in Columbus, Chief Henry E. French, had reported that Franklin Jones was under arrest for a drugstore burglary. An accomplice, though, had told him that the prisoner's real name was Miller. Furthermore, he was wanted in South Carolina for murdering a Columbia policeman.

At that point, Strickland and his colleagues were perplexed by this news. The only local officer slain in the last several years was Henry Frank Brown. According to an eyewitness, on August 12, 1921, a black gunman fatally shot Brown on Park Street. Investigators later ascertained that the likely culprit was Rufus Adams of Bethune, South Carolina. Although Adams's whereabouts had been unknown since that murder, French had stated that his prisoner was white. Consequently, various veteran officers began recalling other long-forgotten cases. Sergeant Perry W. Knox eventually surmised that they might be holding William Edgar "Dock" Miller.

According to the Columbia *Record*, "Dock" Miller was a "former well-known character in local police circles." Knox recalled that he probably had been arrested at least twenty times. In any case, on February 25, 1906, he had severely stabbed Officer Claudius B. Dreher in the left shoulder amidst a violent brawl on Gates Street.

After serving five years for grand assault, Miller had resumed his criminal activities, notably bootlegging. By 1915, he was back within the South Carolina Penitentiary for highway robbery. On August 30, 1916, however, the convict had escaped from a work detail on Two Notch Road. Nothing more had been heard about him for eight years.

Apparently, Miller eventually had made his way to Columbus, Ohio. During a telephone conversation, Chief French promised to mail the prisoner's photograph. A reporter remarked, "Officer Dreher certainly feels confident that he will identify the man who attacked him all those years ago." Accordingly, once the photo arrived, Dreher, as well as several associates identified "Dock" Miller.

Meanwhile, Governor Thomas G. Macleod had dispatched State Constable Thomas A. Barley northward to retrieve the prisoner and the state penitentiary superintendent, A. Malcolm Scarborough, announced that the customary fifty dollar reward would be paid to Chief French. Not surprisingly, the prisoner was in a sullen mood throughout his train journey. A journalist glibly noted, "Miller had very little to say on his way back to South Carolina." Officer Dreher probably had a chuckle, though, while observing his old adversary, in handcuffs, being escorted back to the penitentiary.

And Away He Went

About 7:00 a.m. on February 2, 1914, several regular patrons sauntered into the Star Café at 1312 Main Street. This popular Columbia eatery, operated by Louis G. Kannellos, had been in business for over a decade. Numerous pedestrians usually stopped by for coffee before heading for work. They were surprised, though, that the café was not serving that Monday morning. The primary African American cook, Willie Johnson, emphatically declared that the proprietor had failed to make appearance. Interestingly, Johnson and his two helpers also had found the front door unlocked.

By all accounts, Kannellos, a genial Greek immigrant, had resided in the city for two decades, along with his brother Peter, the proprietor of a fruit store several blocks down the street. Most commentators agreed that the Star Café did a brisk business throughout the year, especially during the daily lunch hours. Unfortunately, however, Louis Kannellos was an inveterate gambler and he was known to be involved with local bootlegging rings. Apparently, he discreetly sold bottles of illegal whiskey sitting within his back storeroom. Local gossips later claimed that Kannellos had begun "skimming" from his restaurant profits to cover heavy gambling debts.

Meanwhile, Kannellos had begun falling behind with his monthly rent payments, as well as other financial obligations. By January 1914, he collectively owed assorted creditors approximately $9,000, a major sum in that period. Furthermore, he had failed to pay his employees for three weeks. Several downtown residents later told police about observing Kannellos driving down Main Street in his Ford touring car the previous evening. He was last spotted about midnight.

When City Detective Fred S. Strickland later headed to Kannellos's apartment at 1427 Main Street, the neighbors said that he had not been home for two days. Furthermore, a black laborer, Harry Carson, told police investigators about helping Kannellos load some kitchen equipment, including a large meat cutter, into a pickup truck that was parked in the alley behind the Star Café. As Sheriff John C. McCain of Richland County noted, "Like a thief in the night, Mr. Kannellos evidently has departed for parts unknown."

Nevertheless, much of the café furniture, including the tables and chairs, had been left upon the premises. He also had not absconded with either the dishware or kitchen utensils. Of course, his erstwhile employees were upset about not receiving their wages.

Consequently, they began appropriating the various items that had been left behind. The Columbia *Record* declared, "These angry folks have already taken everything they are capable of carrying away to satisfy their wage claims."

Floyd Bailey, the dishwasher, was apprehended by Officer William D. Courtney while heading down Lady Street "carrying a sack full of table silverware." As he explained to City Recorder Charles Verner, "I was just taking my due." Although somewhat sympathetic, Verner still found him guilty of petty larceny. Upon failing to pay a $100 fine, Bailey served ninety days on the county chain gang. Several other former employees, caught performing similar thefts, received comparable jail time.

Not surprisingly, common criminals eventually got into the act. About 2:00 a.m. on February 8, Police Sergeant Perry W. Knox arrested Jake Jones, a notorious thief, at the corner of Washington and Marion Streets. At the time of his apprehension, Jones was carrying a small kitchen sink, which contained a leather suitcase full of table linen. Police investigators later determined that all of those objects were from the Star Café. Jones ruefully admitted stealing previously several other missing fixtures, which he already had sold upon the local black market. Meanwhile, during a cursory inspection of the café Sheriff McCain had found several cases of corn whiskey within a side closet, thereby confirming Kannellos's bootlegging connections.

Several weeks later Kannellos was found to be residing in Huntsville, Alabama. The erstwhile proprietor subsequently had sold off all of the equipment that he had removed before departing South Carolina. In order to satisfy Kannellos's respective creditors, the remainder of his property ultimately was sold at public auction. A local butcher, Eugene D. Dent, bought the Star Café's building space for $450—the amount of Kannellos's debt to him.

With a standing arrest warrant in existence, Kannellos apparently did not return to South Carolina for many years. But he managed to stay in touch with several of his local relatives. By 1917,

Sheriff McCain was aware that the café proprietor had moved permanently to Phoenix, Arizona. Meanwhile, Dent long since had moved his successful meat market into the building space once occupied by the Star Café.

Some Notables Visited the Colonia

Perhaps the finest hostelry in Columbia in 1912 was the Colonia Hotel at 1612 Hampton Street. The hotel certainly received some excellent publicity when two celebrities met by chance within the main lobby. About 10:00 a.m. on April 8,1912, the famous national politician William Jennings Bryan encountered Miss Billie Burke, then a popular young stage actress.

The previous afternoon Bryan had arrived in the city aboard a Southern Railways passenger train from Richmond, Virginia. The Democratic Party's presidential candidate in three elections, Bryan possessed a large personal following among South Carolina voters. Throughout the last twenty years the "Great Commoner" had visited Columbia on many occasions. He usually was traveling to Florida where he owned considerable real property. During this stopover, though, he was scheduled to deliver a lecture at the auditorium of the YMCA Building on Main Street. Bryan still was regarded as among the foremost American political orators.

Shortly after arriving in town, numerous pedestrians observed Bryan, carrying a single valise, walking briskly toward the Colonia Hotel. The Columbia *Record* declared, "He presented a strong and manly appearance...and hundreds of admiring spectators were turned upon him." He signed the hotel registry simply as "W.J. Bryan, Lincoln, Nebraska." He remained within the main lobby for several minutes exchanging casual small talk with his well-wishers. He pointedly refused, however, to discuss any national politics with several reporters. Upon dispatching a telegram to a land agent in Jacksonville, Florida, the "Peerless Leader" retired to his fifth floor room.

That evening, at 7:00 p.m., Bryan addressed "the largest gathering ever seen indoors in Columbia." Throughout his remarks the Nebraskan repeatedly excoriated "those vile wretches" supplying liquor to impressionable young American men. "Many times during the course of his address Mr. Bryan was heartily applauded," the *Record* noted.

The next morning Bryan enjoyed a hearty breakfast with several friends within the hotel's dining room. After paying his bill at the front desk, he was about to depart for the train station. At that point, a large boisterous group suddenly entered the Colonia through the main door. They were a theatrical road company on tour with a popular Broadway play, *The Runaway*. Foremost among this assemblage was the comely Billie Burke, a major American stage star. Someone quickly introduced the vivacious blonde actress to Bryan. Consequently, these two notables were obliged to exchange publicly some trivial small talk. After conversing for several minutes, Bryan tipped his brown velour hat and entered a waiting taxi. He was catching a train bound for Daytona, Florida.

With Bryan's departure, the onlookers focused their full attention upon Burke. She cheerily told this impromptu gathering, "This is my first visit to this part of the country, but I have played the South before." Burke did not mention that she had been born in New Orleans. Through extensive vocal coaching, however, the actress had lost her natural southern accent. One journalist declaimed, "She is like the spirit of spring and wherever she is the birds must always want to sing." Another commentator remarked that she demonstrated "a charming childlikeness…that is most refreshing."

Under that beauty, though, there also was a shrewd, sophisticated trouper. The playwright, Michael Martin, had written *The Runaway* to showcase Burke's comedic acting talents. And she had required that a supporting role be created for Hazel Leslie, her close female companion. In order to forestall any adverse gossip, Burke's press agents often highlighted her purported romances with various male actors. During this tour Burke was linked romantically with her English costar, C. Aubrey Smith. He actually was married secretly to another major cast member, Monica Delaney.

This comedy subsequently had a successful run of five days at the Columbia Theater. Billie Burke later enjoyed a lengthy career in movies, radio and television. Of course, she is most famous for her movie role, in 1938, as the "good witch" in *The Wizard of Oz*. This film classic was based upon Frank Baum's satirical novel, which lampooned Bryan's political campaign style. The original "Peerless Leader" was the role model for the egotistical, bombastic wizard. During the shooting perhaps Burke recalled actually meeting Bryan within the Colonia's main lobby back in April 1912.

The Actress and the Cop

In February 1915, an acting company on tour arrived in Columbia to present a drama, *33 Washington Square*, at the Columbia Theater. After a performance run of three nights they headed for another engagement in Augusta, Georgia. For unexplained reasons, though, a member of the supporting cast, twenty-eight-year-old Grace Palmer, remained in the city, assuming lodging within the Berkeley Gresham Hotel at 432 Main Street.

Palmer, a veteran trouper, certainly had traveled widely throughout North America. She willingly told the other lodgers about her many "amorous adventures" while on tour. And she possessed sufficient funds to pay regularly her weekly bill of fifteen dollars. During the next three months she spoke vaguely about returning to her old hometown of Chattanooga, Tennessee. The hotel proprietor, Edwin A. Gresham later recalled that initially she lived quietly, seldom venturing out at night.

During the first week of May, however, Palmer suddenly began to drink heavily. Furthermore, every night she was inviting various men into her third floor room. Not surprisingly, the other paying guests soon were complaining to Gresham about her conduct. Consequently, he warned Palmer to "mend her ways," otherwise she would be evicted.

Nevertheless, on May 19, she started drinking during the late morning. By 4:00 p.m., various eyewitnesses were warning Gresham that the actress was "making a scene" on Gervais Street. About three hours later Palmer staggered into the hotel lobby, where she knocked over an expensive marble vase. While picking up the pieces, Gresham angrily ordered her to move out. After uttering several curses she threw an ashtray at Gresham's head, causing a nasty scalp wound. At that point, the actress ran upstairs to her room.

Meanwhile, Gresham's wife summoned the police to enforce the eviction order. Officers Roland B. Thackham and Charles W. Hedgepath arrived with a patrol wagon. Upon reaching the third floor they encountered Palmer "partially clad in the hallway and told her to go...pack up her belongings." Instead, she promptly went into her room and bolted the door. With little difficulty, however, the officers pushed open the door. Thackham busily was "packing her grip when she suddenly seized a heavy porcelain pitcher" and smashed it over his head. As Thackam staggered across the room the actress also struck him across the face with a large hairbrush. In any case, the stricken officer immediately fell to the floor. A physician later remarked that the "initial blow came within the smallest fraction of proving fatal."

Although she struggled fiercely, Hedgepath finally subdued the actress, with some timely assistance from Police Sergeant Owen Daly. She was transported to the Columbia City Jail on Lincoln Street, where her "drunken frenzy" ended upon being lodged in a cell. Furthermore, the police had confiscated all of her personal possessions. Thackham was taken to Columbia Hospital for emergency medical treatment. He was not able to report for duty for six weeks.

Meanwhile, the next morning Palmer appeared before City Recorder William P. Etchinson. The contrite actress declared, "If I hadn't been drunk, I wouldn't have done it, not for the world." But Recorder Etchinson ordered her held for the next session of Richland County General Sessions Court. Palmer was charged with grand assault, resisting arrest and disorderly conduct. Unable to pay a $500 bond, she spent the next four months within the Richland County Jail. During that interval Palmer's relatives in Tennessee had hired Joel A. McCoy to serve as her attorney.

On September 19, she appeared before Circuit Judge Ernest Moore. Shortly after the jury selection, though, Solicitor William H. Cobb requested that a conference be held within the judge's chamber. During this meeting the opposing attorneys reached a plea bargain. The defendant pled guilty to a charge of attempted manslaughter. She was fined $200, which McCoy immediately paid from funds wired by an anonymous "benefactor" in Chattanooga.

Palmer also agreed to depart immediately from Columbia. While preparing to leave, she was warned by Chief of Police John W. Richardson "not to return here any time soon." Prior to departure all of Palmer's personal belongings were returned to her possession.

Under the watchful eye of City Detective James E. Ford, the actress and her attorney boarded a Southern Railways train bound for Atlanta, Georgia. Initially, she intended to spend several months with her relatives in Tennessee. But Miss Palmer told Detective Ford that she planned eventually to resume her stage career. Doubtless, she later made sure not to join any touring company that included Columbia among its itinerary.

Another Stranded Actress in Trouble

On April 24, 1911, about 4:00 p.m., various bystanders at the Union Train Station noticed an attractive woman, thirty-year-old Miss Marie Maxine, and a young man carrying her luggage. She was hurrying to catch a passenger train bound for Raleigh, North Carolina. A few minutes later, however, this pair was arrested by City Detective James E. Ford. The police had been on the lookout for Maxine since she had departed that morning from the City Hotel without paying her bill.

According to the Columbia *Record* she certainly could "recite a plain, hard luck story." She had been an actress with a touring company that was performing a comedy, *Excuse Me*. But their tour through the Carolinas had proven a financial disaster. Consequently, the company had disbanded on March 15, following a final appearance at the Columbia Theater. Although short of funds, the actress took a room in the City Hotel at 1212 Main Street. She had told the proprietor, Mrs. Lillian A, Kaminer, that her New York City agent would be sending some money within a week.

Initially, Kaminer and other guests were "most taken" with the vivacious actress. A reporter later noted, "She had in her possession numerous pictures and programs in which her name appeared." While showing such items, she regaled acquaintances with countless stories about her diverse stage experiences.

Within three weeks, however, the proprietor began reminding Maxine that her unpaid hotel bill was mounting. "She kept waiting but no money reached her from New York," a reporter related. Despite receiving many desperate telegrams from Columbia, Maxine's agent never came through with any funds. The actress angrily repudiated a suggestion that she seek employment with the brothel madams on Gates Street. Although worldly-wise, Miss Maxine assured everyone that she was "no hooker."

Meanwhile, the actress had gained the ardent devotion of another hotel guest, twenty-five-year-old Richard Arlington, an itinerant barber from Brunswick, Georgia. For several weeks the couple was seen around downtown attending various popular entertainments. The actress did not scruple from using Arlington's infatuation to her advantage when the opportunity arose.

About 7:00 a.m. on April 24, Arlington carried the actress's two suitcases to the rear of the lobby. While another accomplice, Dinah Washington, an African American seamstress, diverted Mrs. Kaminer's attention, the pair made their getaway through the back door. They spent the next several hours hiding out within a friend's house on Laurel Street.

Upon discovering Maxine's departure, Kaminer filed a criminal complaint with the police. Consequently, various officers throughout the day watched for the runaways at the Union Train Depot. An informer had reported that the actress had bought a ticket for Raleigh, where she was planning to join an acting company staging the hit comedy *The Girl in the Taxi*. Following their arrest, though, Maxine and Arlington were lodged within the Richland County Jail.

The next morning the pair appeared before Magistrate James H. Fowles. Besides not paying her large bill, Kaminer claimed that the actress had stolen hotel property, notably several expensive linen towels. Fowles ruled that unless she raised eighty dollars Maxine would be spending the next three months in the county jail. Not surprisingly, her "pathetic, forlorn manner" gained the positive sympathy of numerous spectators. Accordingly, someone literally began "passing the hat" on her behalf. "Several dollars were raised," a reporter wrote, "but the full amount due Mrs. Kaminer remains unpaid." The unhappy actress, therefore, spent the next two days within her jail cell.

By April 27, several friends had managed to raise enough money to satisfy Kaminer. Upon her release, Maxine purchased a train ticket for Atlanta, as well as several personal toilet items. She explained to various acquaintances that her new company now was touring Georgia. The actress told Magistrate Fowles that she was "glad to say 'goodbye' to Columbia where she has had such an unpleasant experience."

Unfortunately, though, a reporter noted that "the gallant youth who had endeavored to assist Miss Maxine…did not fare as well as his friend." Unable to pay a twenty-five dollar fine, Arlington was sentenced to serve a month within the county jail. He already had been evicted from the City Hotel. During that period, however, white prisoners usually were exempt from serving upon the county chain gang. But the barber was expected to provide free barbering to the jail staff. And the actress probably forgot all about her erstwhile beau upon reaching Atlanta. Doubtless, Arlington received no postcards from Miss Maxine telling him about *Girl In the Taxi*. Hopefully, he took such disappointments in stride.

A Body in the River

Two Columbia fishermen, John A. Gaston and Samuel H. McLean, on July 28, 1915, were rowing along the Congaree River, four miles below Hopkins. About 4:00 p.m., they were passing some marshes that for some months had been submerged by heavy rains. A recent dry spell, though, had caused the waters to subside. Consequently, both men readily noticed a suspicious object lying upon an open patch of ground. The fishermen agreed that they probably were viewing a human corpse. The pair quickly reported this grim discovery to Sheriff John S. McCain of Richland County.

Two days later Sheriff McCain, two deputies and Coroner James A. Scott finally reached that death scene on foot. The waters were still too high to make an easy approach to the site. Not surprisingly, they found a badly decomposed body, with some parts already skeletal. Although Coroner Scott discerned that the deceased was male, he could not determine his racial origins. Furthermore, he was not able to establish the man's approximate age. But Scott did know that several months earlier he had died by drowning. The corpse was attired in a flannel blue shirt, work overalls and leather boots. The dead man, however, possessed no identification papers upon his person. The Columbia *Record* noted, "There had been several freshets recently and…the police knew the body might have come many miles up the river."

Meanwhile, they could not recall that any missing person had been reported locally for many months. Some weeks earlier five convicts had escaped from a nearby work camp. But all those convicts long since had been recaptured. As was the prevailing custom, they buried this anonymous person within an unmarked grave in an adjacent meadow. After making fruitless inquiries throughout South Carolina, McCain concluded that person's identity was destined to remain a mystery.

On September 15, William B. Quick of 1006 Whaley Street in Columbia telephoned the sheriff about the case. A carpenter by trade, Quick had been working on a construction project in Winston-Salem, North Carolina, for the past month. Upon returning home, though, Mrs. Annie M. Quick told him about the grisly discovery. The couple was convinced that the unidentified man was their missing son, John R. "Jack" Frick, an army deserter.

According to his father, Jack Frick had been a "restless young man." Upon finishing public school, he initially had worked with his father in the construction business. In April 1912, however, he had enlisted with the U.S. Army. For most of his enlistment period, he had served with Company L of the Fourth Infantry Regiment at Fort Bliss, Texas. But Corporal Frick had come to detest military life. During a furlough in Houston, Texas, in April 1915, he decided to desert. At that point, the U.S. Department of War released a circular offering a $150 reward for his apprehension. Three months afterward a cousin reported seeing him in Brunswick, Georgia, walking through the Southern Railways Depot. The older Quick believed that he had reached Georgia by sneaking rides upon various freight trains. "My son was endeavoring to get home in an indirect way," he concluded. Furthermore, the deserter probably was traversing the Congaree River within a small wooden boat that overturned after encountering some unexpected flooding.

At Quick's request the body was exhumed from the original makeshift grave for further examination. He mentioned that his son possessed a "peculiarly shaped third toe on the right foot," the result of a childhood injury and subsequent surgery. As the *Record* revealed, "The unknown body indeed showed such markings on the toe and foot." Accordingly, Coroner Scott agreed to release those remains to the Quicks' custody for a permanent interment. The dead man ultimately was buried within a Pickens County cemetery.

Convinced that Corporal Quick was dead, military authorities subsequently revoked the reward offer. Some observers, though, still suspected that the resourceful deserter was alive and residing in "parts unknown." Although the United States was two years from entering World War I, perhaps Frick had foreseen that eventuality. He had departed the army while the getting was good.

A Belated Find Along the Congaree

On November 28, 1931, two African American workers were placing some lumber within a shed nearby to Granby Landing upon the Congaree River. About 5:00 p.m., they noticed an empty motorboat floating toward the shore. Upon securing the boat they found on the flooring a raincoat, a pair of oars and a kerosene lantern. At that point, Cliff Donahue declared that the craft belonged to his friend, Louis R. Roberts, a well-known fisherman along the Congaree. But Roberts was nowhere in sight.

By all accounts, Roberts was a native of New Bern, North Carolina. During World War I he had served with the American

Expeditionary Force (AEF) in France. Throughout the 1920s he had made a modest living as a fisherman upon the Congaree River. Accordingly, he augmented his annual income by engaging in fur trapping.

A lifelong bachelor, Roberts had resided within a small cabin several hundred yards adjacent to Granby Landing, "from where he made his excursions upon the river." Although not an actual recluse, he certainly was a private person. Roberts especially was resentful when casual acquaintances inquired about his past. He also was known to range far down both the Wateree and Santee Rivers. He liked, though, to boast about his prowess in hunting alligators.

Donahue recalled watching his friend depart in the boat that morning. Roberts had spoken about heading downriver to check on some fur traps and fish snares. Because the boat clearly had not overturned, several onlookers surmised that Roberts had fallen into the water. Known to be a good swimmer, no one could conceive that the fisherman had drowned. Consequently, someone suggested that Roberts was a victim of foul play. Nevertheless, no witnesses ever came forward to claim that they had seen him during that fateful day.

Early the next morning Sheriff T. Alex Heise of Richland County organized a systematic attempt to recover Roberts's body. The searchers used large nets to drag the channel bottom and also frequently detonated dynamite in order to bring the corpse to the surface. Unfortunately, though, unusually heavy rains, which caused the river to rise, ultimately frustrated all recovery efforts. Veteran river men, including Donahue and Jack Olney, speculated that a strong freshet had swept Roberts's remains far downstream.

By December 13, the victim's brother, William M. Roberts of Lynchburg, Virginia, had arrived to recover the body. He offered a fifty-dollar reward for anyone managing to accomplish that goal. He told the Columbia *Record*, "I'm going to stay here until I find some trace or…I'm sure his body can't be found." Eventually, he hired Olney to assist in the recovery project. Two days later Olney's black assistant, Booker T. Watts, found a cap and glove lying upon a protruding rock, about twelve miles below Granby Landing, but no one could confirm whether those items belonged to Roberts. After ten days of fruitless activity, they gave up the effort.

Nothing more was heard about the missing man until the late afternoon of January 29, 1933. A hunter, Fred Williams, was stalking a deer within a remote locale, approximately seventeen miles south of Columbia. While walking through the woods, some fifty feet from the Congaree, Williams located skeletal human remains upon a pile of driftwood. Within two hours he had managed to telephone Sheriff Heise about his grim discovery.

After some difficulty a recovery party managed to reach the scene. Heise and Coroner John A. Sargeant agreed that they probably were viewing Roberts's remains. High waters likely had carried the corpse ashore to that spot. The coroner readily determined that the skeleton belonged to an adult male. Since he found no evidence of traumatic physical injury, Sargeant concluded that death was due to natural causes.

Roberts probably had fallen overboard after experiencing a fatal heart attack. Enough clothing remained, notably a pair of leather boots, for the victim's nephew, Ellis Roberts, to make a positive identification. Furthermore, the deceased's teeth matched Roberts's surviving dental records.

Eventually, Roberts's remains were interred within a church cemetery in New Bern. His relatives were relieved to know his ultimate fate, while Sheriff Heise was gratified that the case had been solved. Jack Olney told a journalist that the Congaree "sometimes is obliging about revealing its secrets."

He Could Not Reach the Shore

On April 18, 1923, two fishermen, A. Hugo Wolfe and Ernest W. Allen, were riding in a motorboat along the Congaree River within Calhoun County, some twenty miles downstream from Columbia. About 9:00 a.m., they suddenly noticed a badly decomposed corpse in the water tangled up amidst some floating cypress logs. The pair subsequently placed the remains upon a small island situated next to the riverbank and reported their grisly find to Sheriff Frank Hill of Calhoun County. Neither Hill nor his deputies, though, could recall any local persons that had been reported missing within the vicinity of the Congaree during the last several years. Since the body was attired in masculine clothing, they assumed that the deceased had been male. But they could not determine his exact racial identity. Accordingly, Hill circulated a bulletin among his law enforcement colleagues throughout South Carolina. Two days later Sheriff T. Alex Heise of Richland County telephoned to report that he probably knew something about the case.

Nearly three months earlier, on January 12, Alex Richardson of 2219 Rembert Street in Columbia, while strolling down Gervais Street, was spotted by City Detective William T. Kelly. Apparently, Richardson was a prime suspect in several recent burglaries. Despite Kelly's order to stop, he began running toward the Gervais Street Bridge. Within several minutes two patrolmen also had joined the chase. Upon realizing that he would be overtaken on the bridge, Richardson headed directly for the Congaree. The fugitive clearly wanted to swim across the river to New Brookland, where he had many friends.

Several onlookers, however, declared that the water was too cold for swimming. After Richardson began experiencing problems in midstream, he tried to reach some nearby rocks. All the eyewitnesses on the shore "saw him throw up his hands as he sank for the first and only time." No one could recall seeing him appear again upon the surface. They believed that the weight of a heavy brown army overcoat had helped pull down the luckless swimmer. An hour later the victim's cap was found floating near the dock at Granby Landing.

Meanwhile, a search party was attempting to recover Richardson's body. They proceeded to drag the river for several miles below the Gervais Street Bridge. At one point, they repeatedly detonated dynamite in the water, hoping the concussions might cause the corpse to rise to the surface. Interestingly, one explosion did bring up an alligator carcass, measuring five feet in length. But they still did not locate the victim. Sheriff Heise surmised that the Congaree's swift currents already had swept the body southward. Nothing more was heard about the case until Hill's circular appeared in the mail on April 20. That afternoon Sheriff Heise made the long drive to Hill's office in St Mathews.

Sheriff Hill's deputies had discovered that the body's right arm and left leg were missing. Furthermore, most of the clothing long since had been reduced to tatters. But the heavy brown overcoat had remained in fairly good condition. Heise recalled readily that all of the known eyewitnesses had agreed that Richardson was wearing such a garment during his fatal swim. The Columbia *Record* declared, "The coat was the principal factor in the positive identification of the body."

A neighbor subsequently told Heise that the dead man once had mentioned that a brother lived in Chesterfield County. Richardson also had spoken about being a former resident of Wilmington, North Carolina. No relatives, though, ever came forward to claim his body. Consequently, the Calhoun County authorities, following the prevailing custom, buried Richardson by the Congaree River, in close proximity to the exact spot where he initially was found. Quite likely, his unmarked grave remains undisturbed to this day.

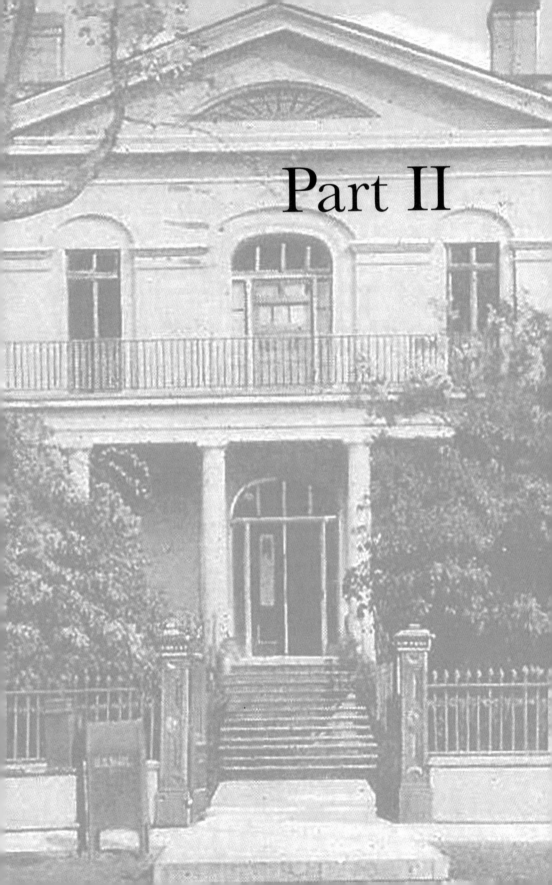

Part II

Much Excitement at Chicora College

During the evening of November 4, 1918, the Columbia police were summoned to William S. Bateman's residence at 1519 Blanding Street. About 10:30 p.m., an intruder had entered the house through a side window while the family was sleeping. They were awakened, however, after he inadvertently knocked over some parlor furniture. This unknown visitor was "long gone" by the time any officers reached the scene. A neighbor reported observing a man exiting Bateman's house through the back door. He was last seen running swiftly down Marion Street toward Elmwood Avenue. Although three eyewitnesses agreed that the man was white, they did not provide much else in the way of a good physical description Accordingly, City Detectives Robert Broome and James E. Ford were returning to their automobile when they noticed a young African American male approaching on a bicycle. They promptly identified him as eighteen-year-old Will Montgomery, a suspect in several robberies. This unforeseen encounter precipitated some noisy excitement for the surrounding neighborhood.

While still a teenager, Montgomery already was well known to local lawmen. For several years he had been utilizing the alias of "Dewey McCreary" around town. He was believed to be the ringleader of a street gang operating within the Waverly section. Doubtless, Montgomery was aware that the police for looking for him. As the Columbia *Record* declared, "The young negro [*sic*] seeing there was trouble ahead, leaped from the cycle and made his break." Montgomery later admitted that he was riding on a stolen bicycle. With the detectives in close pursuit, he quickly reached the campus of Chicora College, a female educational institution at 1605 Blanding Street. The nimble fugitive easily scaled the wall surrounding the school grounds. Being thick with ornamental shrubbery the campus "made an excellent place for playing hide and seek with the police."

The officers, though, summoned the night watchman, John Elwood, to open the front gate. Suspecting that Montgomery was armed, the pair entered the campus with drawn revolvers. Meanwhile, the fugitive had found concealment within the heavy foliage. All the commotion thoroughly frightened Chicora's staff and student residents. Amidst this dragnet a "thrilling moment" occurred after Ford finally noticed his quarry hiding beneath a large shrub. The fleet youth promptly dashed toward a nearby tree grove. In order to summon his partner, Ford fired twice in the air. President Samuel E. Byrd finally emerged from his residence to demand an explanation from the officers. Although still attired in his nightshirt, Byrd also had managed to pull on a pair of trousers. "In the meantime the entire neighborhood was highly excited by the gunfire," the *Record* noted. And Montgomery again was nowhere in sight.

A student began yelling that she had seen him running into the campus garage. As the detectives entered through the front door, Montgomery dove headfirst out a closed window "thereby taking the blind, sash, and window with him." He was rendered senseless when his skull subsequently struck a brick walkway. Moreover, he was cut badly by all of the broken glass. A bloody, dazed Montgomery was sprawled upon the ground, unable to stand on his feet.

Complying with Ford's request, President Byrd had telephoned police headquarters to summon a patrol wagon. Upon reaching the college that vehicle had parked on Blanding Street in front of the main gate. A large crowd was watching as several officers carried the bleeding prisoner out on a stretcher. Many of these onlookers assumed the detectives had shot Montgomery. The following morning a rumor was circulating around town that he was dead. Chief of Police John W. Richardson encountered much skepticism when he attempted to refute such false reports.

The prisoner actually had received emergency medical treatment at the Good Samaritan Hospital. He later was lodged within the Richland County Jail. Although Montgomery had been implicated in a dozen robberies, he was not a suspect in the failed burglary at Bateman's house. The exact identity of that culprit never was ascertained by investigators. City Recorder Charles W. Kimball ordered that Montgomery be held for trial in Richland County General Sessions Court. Ultimately, he was sentenced to serve five years within the state penitentiary. The convict likely was too busy laboring on a chain gang to recall all of the commotion that he had brought to Chicora College, as well as that quiet Blanding Street neighborhood.

When Dr. Buzzard Came Calling

In August 1922, Chief Fred S. Strickland was told by some reliable contacts that a notorious African American character, Thomas Nelson, was back in Columbia. This wily operator, known within the black community as "Dr. Buzzard," was a self-styled "root doctor." He professed to possess various magical mystery potions, capable of healing any ailment. The local police, though, believed that he was merely a slick grifter. Upon receiving this news, Chief Strickland advised his men to be vigilant for "Dr. Buzzard."

A native of Johns Island, Nelson traveled widely throughout the Carolinas. A reporter noted that he routinely peddled his remedies, especially among Lowcountry migrants. Nelson also boasted that he often dealt with "patients" residing as far north as New York City, who traveled southward specifically to gain his medical services. Although many root doctors genuinely were well versed in traditional folk medicines, Nelson apparently was a blatant con artist. During his last visit to Columbia, in 1920, he had been arrested for vagrancy. And he was a known associate of bootleggers operating in Arthur Town, a black hamlet just beyond the city limits along Bluff Road. Consequently, several of his "wonderful potions" were laced liberally with corn whiskey.

Upon arriving in Columbia he had circulated around the various black neighborhoods to ascertain which households contained sickly persons. As the Columbia *Record* wrote, "Witnesses testified he always approached such houses and inquired if all was well." Mrs. Daisy Jordan of 702 Pendleton Street had told him about some severe arthritic soreness in her right ankle. Accordingly, he sold her an ointment guaranteed to relieve the pain. She borrowed ten dollars from her brother to pay Nelson's fee. But he had provided her with a mixture of camphor and gasoline. Upon applying this concoction to her leg, the woman's skin began to peel badly. Not surprisingly, her enraged husband, William Jordan, went looking for "Dr. Buzzard" with a loaded shotgun.

Meanwhile, Nelson had learned that Mrs. Maggie Joyce of 1406 Taylor Street was suffering from chronic bronchitis. He blithely assured her that she had become bewitched "after some dark-skinned woman had thrown magic dust on her clothing." Thereupon, she was sold a pint of corn liquor mixed with gasoline. But this time an irate spouse, Garfield Joyce, took his complaint to the police.

After making some inquiries, Police Sergeant J. Walter Hite discovered that Nelson was residing in Mrs. Hattie Hall's boardinghouse at 1209 Assembly Street. About 7:00 p.m. on September 4, Hite and two patrolmen went there to apprehend the root doctor. Apparently, though, someone had warned him that they were on the way. A getaway was thwarted when they caught Nelson climbing out a rear window. A search of his room produced a steamer trunk containing several pint fruit jars, full of corn whiskey. He subsequently was lodged within the Columbia City Jail.

On September 6, he was brought before City Recorder Charles J. Kimball. Ten of Nelson's "patients" appeared to render "vigorous testimony" against him. "All in all, the witnesses made out a bad case against Nelson," the *Record* noted, "in spite of his protests that he was 'called in' on the cases." He also claimed to be guarding that trunk for a friend, totally unaware of its illegal contents.

Recorder Kimball decided "to hand a hard jolt" to the defendant. He was declared guilty of petty fraud, practicing medicine without a license, and bootlegging. Unable to pay a $500 fine, "Dr. Buzzard" was given five months upon the county chain gang. Furthermore, after completing that sentence, he was expected to depart from Columbia. Otherwise, he would be arrested promptly for vagrancy and spend more time working on some Richland County roadway.

Doubtless, five months later he wasted little time catching a train for another city. Other African American root doctors continued to peddle their items around town. But local residents probably saw nothing more of "Dr. Buzzard" for a long time.

The Faith Healer Had No Luck

For several days in February 1933, a notable African American "divine healer," Luther Russell, had been visiting with old friends in Columbia. During this stay he also had conducted three "healing services" in Mount Hebron Baptist Church at 1310 Sumter Street. Quite early in the morning, on February 12, he was summoned to provide "divine assistance" to Henry T. Holloway, a critically ill man in Orangeburg, South Carolina. On this sojourn, though, Russell never managed to reach his destination.

By all accounts, Russell was well known among black Baptists throughout the Carolinas. He had been undertaking faith healing activities for fifteen years. Otherwise, he regularly was employed as a street sanitation worker in Asheville, North Carolina. Apparently, he had made numerous trips to Columbia during that period. While in the city he usually was assisted by Ernest Green, a local lay Baptist preacher. Several of Russell's admirers later stated he had "achieved many miraculous cures through blind faith." But a prominent black Columbian, Seymour Carroll, assured a reporter that Russell's various successes were achieved "through sheer dumb luck."

About 6:15 a.m., Russell and three companions climbed into Green's green Oldsmobile sedan, bound for Orangeburg. Green was at the wheel and the patient's brother, James Holloway, went along to provide accurate travel directions. Rounding out the quartet was Holloway's wife, Gertie. In any case, at 7:00 a.m., Green's speeding automobile was heading southward along the Orangeburg Highway, approximately fifteen miles below Columbia. At that point, his left front tire suddenly was punctured by a sharp object lying upon the roadway. Accordingly, Green lost control and the auto headed toward an adjacent pasture. The vehicle "turned turtle" three times before crashing into a vacant wooden shack. As the Columbia *Record* declared, "The automobile was completely demolished, beyond all repair."

Meanwhile, several onlookers assisted in removing the unconscious Russell from the wreckage. Although they had received numerous bruises, the other three occupants escaped serious injury. A local white storekeeper, Joseph Wright, agreed to loan his car for the conveyance of the comatose faith healer to the Good Samaritan Hospital in Columbia. Prevailing racial etiquette, however, precluded that Wright personally would be transporting the African Americans within his automobile. Consequently, Wright's black helper, James Norseworthy, was hired to drive them to the hospital. Three hours after arriving in the emergency room, Russell died from major injuries to his skull, as well as various vital internal organs.

Russell's corpse subsequently was transferred into the custody of a local African American undertaker, William C. Champion, whose parlor stood at 701 Richland Street. With Sheriff T. Alex Heise of Richland County observing, the mortician began sorting out Russell's personal effects. They agreed that faith healing must have been lucrative, because seventy-five dollars in cash was found within his wallet. A reporter added, "In his pockets there also were cigarettes, a prayer book, and a rabbit's foot." Heise remarked that this last object definitely had not afforded him much protection.

The following morning the victim's son, Floyd Russell, arrived to claim the body. He ultimately was buried within an Asheville church cemetery. Furthermore, Russell's untimely passing caused considerable regret around the Carolinas. In essence, no one had been able to render "divine treatment" upon his stricken body. Meanwhile, Henry T. Holloway's ultimate fate went unrecorded in the press accounts of this accident.

They Got the Wrong Fellow

About 2:00 p.m. on February 21, 1920, Chief of Police John W. Richardson in Columbia received an urgent telegram from Greenville, South Carolina. Several hours earlier a notorious African American desperado, Joe Turner, had shot two policemen during a shootout. One of the officers eventually died from his wounds. The officers had disrupted an armed holdup in progress at a downtown pharmacy. Despite an extensive dragnet, though, the resourceful bandit had evaded capture. His pursuers believed that the fugitive had fled the city aboard a passing freight train. Throughout the next week there were many purported sightings of him throughout South Carolina. For several hours on February 22, the Columbia police were convinced that they had nabbed the outlaw.

A career criminal, thirty-five-year-old Turner was known to be a violent, dangerous man. Five months before the killing he had been released from the South Carolina Penitentiary, after serving eight years for armed robbery. He was described as a "medium sized, stocky, and ginger colored negro [*sic*] man." And Turner had boasted to friends that he would not be captured alive. As the Columbia *Record* observed, "Something like a dozen negroes [*sic*] are being held in different parts of the state, but none so far has been positively identified." Not surprisingly, the Greenville authorities had posted a $500 reward for his capture, dead or alive.

Meanwhile, James H. Gilbert, a Southern Railways conductor, was on a passenger train heading from Columbia toward Union at about 7:00 p.m. Approximately six miles out of Columbia he noticed three black hoboes riding within an open boxcar upon a passing freight train. He noted that one of these transients apparently bore a resemblance to the fugitive.

During a brief stopover at Frost Station, Gilbert telephoned Chief Richardson about his suspicions. Subsequently, Deputy Sheriff T. Alex Heise of Richland County drove his car to the railroad crossing at Broad River Road, in order to confirm Gilbert's observation. Heise quickly concluded that the conductor's hunch probably was accurate.

At that point, Chief Detective Fred S. Strickland led several officers to the Blanding Street crossing to intercept the train. As the locomotive reached that spot "the negroes saw the officers in waiting and jumped off." Although two of the hoboes successfully escaped, they did capture their main quarry. The fugitive was running north on Blanding Street when he literally ran into Patrolman Michael C. Turbeville. The officers agreed that he certainly matched Turner's general description. The man insisted that he was Reuben Royall of Lanes, South Carolina.

Initially, he claimed to be a member of a Southern Railways labor gang working on damaged track several miles north of Columbia. Their foreman had arranged for Royall and two other laborers to ride back to Columbia aboard that train. Strickland, however, curtly dismissed that contention because Royall was "wearing two pairs of pants, two flannel shirts, and other extra clothing." He also had a burlap sack containing many personal items, including a gold pocket watch.

Royall eventually admitted that he had been traveling in that boxcar from Spartanburg, South Carolina. The transient claimed

REMEMBERING COLUMBIA, SOUTH CAROLINA

to be bound for Savannah, Georgia, where a steady job was pending. He vehemently denied any knowledge either of Turner or the shootings. After being lodged in the Richland County Jail, his photograph was relayed to Greenville. But Sheriff Sam D. Willis wired back that the prisoner definitely was not Turner.

Despite the massive manhunt, Turner successfully left South Carolina. On February 28, he was seen riding upon a trolley in Charlotte, North Carolina. He disappeared from sight, however, before the police could make an arrest. Several days later the desperado evidently took part in an armed robbery near Beckley, West Virginia. And he remained among the missing for the next two months. By May 9, he finally was under arrest in Lynchburg, Virginia. He was captured after murdering a storekeeper during an abortive holdup. Turner was executed on August 18, 1920, within the Virginia State Penitentiary in Richmond.

And Reuben Royall did not enjoy a pleasant stay in Columbia. Chief Richardson had circulated his picture with other lawmen around South Carolina, but he apparently was not wanted by any other municipality. Nevertheless, Richardson decided to hold him on a vagrancy charge. Unable to pay a fine of thirty dollars, on February 26, City Recorder Charles J. Kimball sentenced him to serve a month upon the county chain gang. Five days later, Royall and several confederates escaped from a work detail on Garner's Ferry Road. Unfortunately for Royall, though, he was recaptured within three hours. Consequently, that escapade cost him another five months of freedom. At least he fared better than the late Joe Turner.

Passing Away in Complete Loneliness

Many pedestrians were complaining that some "repugnant odors" were coming from a vacant warehouse at 604 Lady Street. By April 12, 1927, this noxious smell had been emanating for three weeks from the building, once the Columbia Petroleum Company's main warehouse. Eventually, two nearby residents, James W. Dorn and John M. Mooneyman, were demanding that the police probe this obvious public nuisance. About 9:00 a.m. on April 12, Police Sergeant James E. Taylor and Officer Louis Knox went over to investigate the complaint. Upon entering the edifice they found a decomposed human corpse within a small storeroom. The Columbia *Record* noted, "The officers inadvertently had encountered the final resting place of an unknown man."

They also noticed that the front warehouse door was fastened from the inside. The body was clad in a faded blue serge suit, containing no identifying labels. Furthermore, he had been wearing a battered straw hat. And the deceased had carried no personal papers that could establish his specific identity. Within his jacket pocket, however, they found a sharp razor, wrapped in brown paper. Lying upon an adjacent crate was an old train schedule, with the word "Florida" scrawled at the top.

Because no bloodstains were in evidence, the investigators dismissed any notion of foul play. Due to advanced decomposition, moreover, Coroner William A. McCain of Richland County was unable to ascertain the dead man's approximate age, as well as racial identity. McCain did conclude that he had been deceased for two months. Various commentators agreed that he probably was a rootless "floater" passing through the Carolinas bound for Florida.

Quite likely, he regularly had traveled toward his destinations aboard any available freight train. Apparently, the hobo had picked the padlock upon the main warehouse doorway. Because the police had found an empty whiskey bottle by the body, a reporter speculated that the sojourner "was drunk while he sought out shelter." Before retiring for the night, he had fastened the door from the inside.

Upon settling within the storeroom, the tramp took it easy, with his back propped against the outer wall. Moreover, he had sought warmth by starting a fire in a small straw pile. In any case, the officers had noticed that several matches were lying about the floor. And he had secured a couple of large burlap sacks for covering. During his sleep the hobo subsequently had passed away. Accordingly, the police found the body still leaning against the wall, with the head tilted slightly to the left. This resourceful intruder probably had sought out that vacant building one cold February night. Chief of Police Fred S. Strickland could not recall that any local man had been reported missing for the last six months. Meanwhile, Fire Chief A. McCraney Marsh had announced that after a routine inspection in September 1926, his men had found the building in "good order."

Not surprisingly, reports about this grisly business had spread throughout the downtown. As the *Record* proclaimed, "Hundreds of Columbians soon congregated…getting as near as they could to the gruesome find." Later that afternoon Coroner McCain placed the remains within a plain wooden coffin. The deceased ultimately was interred in an unmarked grave amidst the "potters' field" section of Elmwood Cemetery. Apparently, no graveside religious rites accompanied the burial.

All public interest in this case faded completely within a few days, and the man's actual identity never was ascertained by police investigators. "Most likely he was a wanderer," a reporter concluded, "who disappeared from his hometown in another state and was never found again." Consequently, he died in complete solitude, with no loved ones to mourn his passing.

He Wanted Some Stability

By September 1932, Alex Chaffin had been a homeless drifter for approximately two years. The erstwhile white textile worker from Gastonia, North Carolina, arrived "in hobo style" aboard a Seaboard Air Line Railway freight train on September 12. Chaffin later claimed that he intentionally sought to get arrested. And he accomplished that goal within three hours.

Apparently, the tramp made his exit from a boxcar about 2:00 a.m., nearby to the Blanding Street crossing. For the next couple hours Chaffin wandered through the downtown, totally deserted at that early hour. By 4:30 a.m. he had decided to break into the Cameron Drug Store at 1003 Whaley Street. Not surprisingly, a neighbor, Charles Senn, could hear him "messing around" within the pharmacy. Sensing that a robbery was in progress, Senn quickly summoned the police by telephone. City Detective Rowland McCallister and Officer William L. Gambrell were dispatched to the scene.

Upon encountering the burglar inside the store they arrested him with no trouble. The Columbia *Record* added, "In the intruder's pockets, the officers found razor blades, several knives, and some cigarettes." Interestingly, he had made no effort to steal any of the pharmacy's prescription merchandise. During a subsequent inspection at the Columbia City Jail, Police Sergeant E.D. Harrell also found a pair of glasscutters within Chaffin's right boot. He cheerfully told police that he was seeking "to get into trouble in order to have a place to eat and sleep." Chafflin thoroughly was tired of residing within the over-crowded "hobo jungles," so common amidst the Great Depression.

At 11:00 a.m. the prisoner made an appearance before City Recorder Heyward Brockington. Although admitting to having "done time" in Macon, Georgia, for "receiving stolen goods," he denied being a common criminal. He was charged with petty larceny and unlawful housebreaking. But Chaffin hotly disputed that second charge by claiming that he had entered the store through an unlocked front door. In any case, the pharmacist, Dr. James B. Cameron, indignantly repudiated this assertion. The city recorder, meanwhile, curtly dismissed Chaffin's "quaint argument."

Unable to post a $1,000 bond, Chaffin was lodged within the Columbia County Jail to await trial. He managed to secure John Hughes Cooper as his attorney. Two months later he was tried on the unlawful entry charge in the Richland County General Sessions Court. After being found guilty, Circuit Judge Mendel L. Smith sentenced him to spend two years within the South Carolina Penitentiary. Upon concluding that sentence, moreover, the prisoner was required to depart promptly from the state. Otherwise, he would serve time for vagrancy on the Richland County chain gang.

Doubtless, Chaffin had not anticipated having to spend such a lengthy stay in Columbia. He bitterly complained to spectators that Judge Smith was "making an example out of him." Nevertheless, he had secured free room and board for the duration.

A Most Mysterious Killing

Quite early one Saturday morning, on October 14, 1917, James A. "Jack" Scott, the Richland County coroner, left his home to go hunting. Before departing Scott told his wife, Cenie, that he would be returning around sundown. His usual companion on such excursions was Rural Officer Jesse N. Helms, a close friend for many years. Incredibly, however, they became involved in a personal shootout that evening, resulting in Scott's death.

By 1917, Scott was serving out his third term as the county coroner. He resided in a large house standing adjacent to the state fairgrounds. He belonged to various local social clubs and "possessed a large circle of friends around town." Furthermore, Scott was an influential figure within the South Carolina Democratic Party. The Columbia *Record* observed that Helms had been an "efficient" rural policemen for twelve years. "He has a good, clean record as a police officer," a reporter added. And it was common knowledge around Columbia that Helms owed his position to Scott's formidable political connections. Helms resided with his family at 3819 Wheat Street. Interestingly, no observer could recall a single instance of trouble between these two old friends.

The hunters stalked small game within the vicinity of Hopkins for most of the day. Around 4:00 p.m., they climbed into Scott's Dodge coupe for the drive back along Bluff Road toward Columbia. They stopped briefly at a local farm to inspect an automobile that Scott intended to purchase. For no apparent reason, though, they decided to make a stopover in Arthur Town, a rural African American hamlet. Moreover, they sauntered into a grocery store owned by Thomas Blakely, a hard-working black entrepreneur. Due to numerous past visits, Blakely certainly knew both men well. According to Blakely the two white officials "made themselves right at home upon a couple wooden chairs."

They initially sat around drinking from bottles of Cherro-Cola, a popular soft drink. About 6:00 p.m., Scott dispatched Blakely's son to "procure some liquor from a local blind tiger [bootlegger]." He later returned with two quarts of corn whiskey, which the two whites consumed heavily for the next several hours. "As far as I can tell," Blakely recalled, "they just laughed and joked with each other the whole time." In fact, their jokes became so lewd that the grocer felt compelled to send his teenage granddaughter back home. She usually helped him close up the store. Perhaps Blakely had discerned that the drunken men were directing amorous stares in her direction. In any case, both were "considerably under the influence from all that liquor" by midnight.

Upon bidding their host goodbye, they staggered out into the darkness. For an unknown reason, however, the intoxicated men began arguing in loud voices beside Scott's car. Various eyewitnesses agreed that their noisy quarrel continued for approximately ten minutes. At that point, they decided to settle the dispute with gunfire. Accordingly, assorted Arthur Town residents witnessed two prominent white men stage a deadly duel upon the roadway. Before collapsing, Scott managed to fire twice from his .32-caliber Smith & Wesson revolver, whereas his adversary fired six shots with a .38-caliber military pistol, with two bullets hitting the mark. The first cartridge ripped through Scott's left knee, while the other penetrated under the right arm. The Columbia *Record* wrote, "The second shot went clear through Mr. Scott's body, coming out on the left side, just above the hip." He died within minutes of receiving this mortal wound. But Helms only suffered a painful "flesh laceration" upon the left shoulder.

Meanwhile, Blakely called Sheriff John C. McCain to report this bloody episode. The storekeeper clearly had heard Helms mutter, "I didn't want to do it, but he made me. I had no choice." About forty minutes later a quiescent Helms surrendered to McCain and Chief Deputy T. Alex Heise. "The body of the dead man lying on the road surely made a gruesome sight," the *Record* declared. Furthermore, the investigators did not gain much solid information from the bystanders. A disgusted reporter complained, "Although a number of negroes [*sic*] had gathered at the scene, none were inclined to talk or give any account of this difficulty." For instance, Blakely claimed that he had not observed the actual shooting.

Although Helms spent the night in the Richland County Jail, he was released the following afternoon, in lieu of $5,000 bond. By November 4, the county grand jury had indicted him on a charge of second-degree murder. He was brought to trial on January 10, 1918, in Richland County General Sessions Court. When the jury failed to reach a verdict, a mistrial was about to be declared. At that point, Helm's attorney, Lang D. Jennings, managed to have the charge reduced to manslaughter. Accordingly, Helms was sentenced to serve eight years in the South Carolina Penitentiary. He was free on parole, though, within three years. Not surprisingly, a myriad of rumors about this mysterious episode circulated statewide for years. But no plausible official explanation for the deadly duel ever was extended to the public. Clearly there were some things better left unsaid.

Another Baffling Killing

About 4:00 p.m. on November 26, 1918, a prominent Richland County landlord, Patrick Devereaux, sought out Will Johnson, his former sharecropper. Several of Johnson's neighbors were reporting that they had not seen him for over two weeks. Devereaux quickly observed large bloodstains upon the front steps of Johnson's wooden cabin. Furthermore, Johnson did not respond to his persistent knocking. Upon looking through the window he spotted a corpse sprawled on the floor.

An efficient, dependable worker, Johnson had labored for farmers throughout lower Richland County for a decade. During the last five years he had resided on a farm formerly owned by Devereaux. But that acreage now was part of the Camp Jackson reservation. Moreover, the cabin stood within sight of the Heathwood-Camden Road, approximately six miles from Columbia.

Two hours later Sheriff John C. McCain and county Coroner J. Blakely Scott had reached the crime scene. They found two bullets in the victim's upper chest, having been shot at close range by a .45-caliber revolver. The killer also had slashed Johnson's throat "from ear to ear." Scott estimated that he had been dead for about ten days. The investigators made another curious discovery. As the Columbia *Record* noted, "The body was stripped of all clothes, but a blanket was thrown across its upper portions."

But they could not come up with an obvious murder motive. Johnson was not known to possess valuable items and did not carry cash on his person. Sheriff McCain, however, did notice a bankbook sitting upon a small table. He later found out that the deceased had deposited $200 with the Palmetto National Bank in Columbia. Nevertheless, he had not drawn on that checking account for many months. The *Record* declared, "The murderer left no clues and Richland County…has another murder mystery added to its history."

During the investigation Rural Officer James H. Thomas discovered that three weeks earlier a well-dressed black man had been inquiring about the victim along Garner's Ferry Road. Although the stranger said his name was Coleman Mabon, he had not shared any other personal information. Police investigators, however, did not gain any further knowledge about Mabon, especially his subsequent activities. Meanwhile, the sheriff connected Johnson personally to another mysterious story.

Earlier that autumn Johnson had been picking cotton near Hopkins, especially on a farm recently purchased by Joseph St. Mary. This white entrepreneur had told some business associates that he was from Plymouth, North Carolina. Various eyewitnesses recalled observing Johnson repeatedly driving his employer's wagon along Bluff Road heading toward Columbia. Before his sudden departure in late October, St. Mary had failed to pay a hefty rent bill at Mrs. Martha Lucas's boardinghouse at 1314 Lady Street. And he had not been seen locally since that time.

Apparently, though, St. Mary had stored a sizeable amount of cotton within the Columbia Compress Company's warehouse at 815 Devine Street. The manager, William H. Jeffords, stated that St. Mary had deposited 160 bales of quality cotton, along with 931 bales of "burnt cotton." All of this valuable property had remained in storage for six months. By April 1919, he owed the warehouse $7,637 in costs. And Jeffords told reporters that the "quality" cotton was worth $7,800 on the open market, whereas, the damaged commodities still could be sold for $5,000. "Despite an extensive inquiry nothing can be learned of Mr. St. Mary's present whereabouts," the *Record* added. Accordingly, on April 17, the Columbia Compress Company sold off the cotton at public auction.

Not surprisingly, no tangible evidence positively connected St. Mary's disappearance with the brutal murder. Furthermore, the police were unable to ascertain whether Coleman was an actual suspect in the case. In essence, however, these apparent coincidences provided a mysterious element to Johnson's slaying, which never was solved.

The Soldier Fired His Rifle

At 9:00 p.m. on January 28, 1920, First Lieutenant Peter D. Fowler was placed in command of an armed detail of five soldiers from Camp Jackson. Their assignment was to erect a military roadblock upon Garner's Ferry Road, approximately two miles from their cantonment. Fowler and his patrol were expected to apprehend two deserters traveling by automobile from Hopkins into Columbia. The troops, armed with rifles, did not relish this assignment, because the weather was cold. Accordingly, they had been drinking liquor heavily before going on that assignment. Like many other Camp Jackson soldiers, moreover, these patrollers "appeared to be carrying a grudge against the local citizenry." During the last several months several major brawls had occurred between the troops and local civilian rowdies. In any case, Fowler's men apparently were looking for trouble that evening.

Meanwhile, M. Chapell Heath, a prominent cotton broker, was hosting a supper party at his home near Blythewood. Among his guests was thirty-eight-year-old William S. Chaplain of 1126 Elmwood Avenue in Columbia. A Rock Hill native, Chaplain had been superintendent of Draughton's Practical Business College for six years. This popular bachelor usually attended most of the major social events around Richland County. For this gathering Chaplain was serving as Mrs. Lila Aughtry's escort.

By 10:30 p.m., the couple had left the party in an Oldsmobile touring car driven by Charles W. Rice, a civil engineer from

Columbia. Another companion was Walter Bailey, a well-known local attorney. Following a short stopover in Eastover, Rice had started driving westward along Garner's Ferry Road. The ride was proceeding smoothly until 11:30 p.m., when they unexpectedly encountered that military blockade.

About 11:00 p.m., the patrollers had halted a taxicab driven by Henry Ruff, a black cabbie who resided at 1614 Lady Street in Columbia. One of the drunken soldiers had declared loudly that any African American they found "will be catching hell tonight." In any case, Private Raymond Juarez promptly shot out Huff's rear window. As the Columbia *Record* wrote, "The negro [sic] left the cab to run for it and this certainly saved his life." As Ruff made his getaway the inebriated soldiers began slashing the taxi tires with their bayonets.

Thirty minutes later Fowler halted Rice's vehicle by firing his revolver into the air. Upon making a cursory inspection of the car, Fowler brusquely ordered Rice to proceed without delay. He was moving away in low gear "when a bullet was fired point blank through the rear window." A reporter added, "The bullet struck Mr. Chaplain in the small of the back, beneath the left shoulder." And Mrs. Aughtry, covered with Chaplain's blood, lapsed into hysterics. The victim was dead long before any medical assistance could reach the scene. Coroner J. Blakely Scott of Richland County later declared that Chaplain had died "instantly" after being shot. Within a couple days police investigators were told that Private Peyton "Duke" Saunders was the likely shooter.

By 12:30 p.m., Sheriff John C. McCain and Coroner Scott had arrived to mount an investigation. Scott provided Mrs. Aughtry with a strong sedative. Correspondingly, Chaplain's remains were turned over to James W. McCormick, a local undertaker. The body subsequently was conveyed by train to Rock Hill for interment.

Military police already had arrested the entire detail, including Lieutenant Fowler, and placed them within the Camp Jackson

Stockade. As was customary in cases involving military personnel, Sheriff McCain did not attempt to take the culprits into custody. Neither did he demand that they be transferred to the Richland County Jail. A month later, however, he was incensed to learn that the prisoners had been moved secretly to Camp Bragg, North Carolina. Moreover, Fowler and two other suspects had been freed.

Despite numerous assurances, the U.S. Department of War never allowed any of those soldiers to be tried for second-degree murder in Richland County General Sessions Court. Consequently, no one was ever prosecuted for Chaplain's death. A journalist angrily declaimed that the shooting had caused "great enmity against Camp Jackson" throughout the local vicinity. "It is feared that many months will have to pass before this painful sore heals," he added. Five weeks later, on March 5, this "bad blood" certainly intensified when Patrolman Hampton N. Boykin fatally shot Corporal Frank Yonce at the Seaboard Air Line Depot in Columbia. Within a year, however, Secretary of War Newton D. Baker had decided that Camp Jackson would be closed for the foreseeable future. At that point, most of the troops long since had departed from Columbia.

Encountering Some Soldier Highwaymen

About 9:00 a.m. on July 28, 1921, John R. Martin started his usual workday as the traveling salesman for the Flanigan-Clement Company, a wholesale firm located at 927 Gervais Street in Columbia. He was scheduled to make some deliveries to local customers within the company's green Essex roadster. Many local residents easily recognized this vehicle because the company emblem was painted on the right door. Having completed his itinerary by 3:30 p.m., Martin was driving along a rural roadway in Lexington County, bound for Columbia. Martin did not realize that he was "about to have a thrilling experience to tell his friends."

The salesman was two miles from the Broad River when he noticed that a Ford touring car was straddling the road. He recalled encountering this vehicle at a crossroads ten minutes earlier. Two white soldiers, in full uniform, were standing in front of the automobile. With their hands they were beckoning for him to stop. A third soldier brandishing a Winchester rifle suddenly emerged from some roadside foliage. His two confederates also had drawn .45-caliber revolvers. Martin noticed that there were no dwellings along this isolated stretch of road.

The Columbia *Record* declared, "The next chapter was the usual sequel, the bandits going though the pockets and stealing over $75 in cash." Virtually all of these funds belonged to Martin's employers. Although no cars appeared during the heist, the victim did observe an African American man crossing over a nearby field on horseback. Upon realizing that a robbery was in progress, however, the horseman swiftly rode away.

For good measure, the thieves also stole Martin's "gold pocket watch, its chain, his pipe, and practically every other article…on his person." He later told police that most of the robbery occurred in utter silence. Furthermore, Martin did not recognize any of the bandits. The apparent ringleader was a "stocky, swarthy complexioned fellow, with a northern accent." He pointedly warned the salesman not to follow them "under any circumstance." While backing away, he deliberately took direct aim at Martin's head. Sitting within the back seat, another desperado kept pointing his pistol "as long as the two vehicles remained in sight of each other." After they were gone, the shaken victim promptly drove to Columbia, where he reported the crime to Sheriff T. Alex Heise of Richland County.

Because the robbery had occurred within Lexington County, Heise turned the investigation over to Sheriff Austin Roof. The two lawmen agreed that a series of similar daytime holdups had been occurring within both counties during recent months. Meanwhile, an identical highway robbery was reported the following day in Barnwell County. Police investigators did not believe the culprits were stationed at Camp Jackson. Heise guessed that they were "bogus troopers" passing through South Carolina.

In any event, this particular crime never was solved. And such daring highway robberies remained all too common around the state. Accordingly, Martin told friends that he was intending to carry a loaded revolver while making any rural deliveries.

He Became Too Amorous

About 8:00 p.m. on April 22, 1923, thirty-six-year-old Jesse Jones of 913 Pulaski Street bid farewell to several friends. The burly African American locomotive fireman had been spending several pleasant hours in an Assembly Street poolroom. The next morning he was scheduled to commence a Southern Railways run to Richmond, Virginia. Within two hours, however, Jones would be shot fatally in his bedroom.

By all accounts, Jones shared a house with his aged father, Charles Jones, who once had held a similar position with the Atlantic Coast Line Railroad. Although the elder man was a well-respected figure around the neighborhood, the son had a reputation for being quarrelsome, especially when drunk. But he did not have an arrest record with the local police. Nevertheless, around 10:00 p.m., the neighbors suddenly heard a loud gunshot emanating from the Jones residence. Consequently, someone summoned the police over the telephone.

City Detective Shovine S. Shorter and Sergeant Perry W. Knox were the first officers to reach the scene. They discovered the younger Jones's bloody body sprawled upon the bedroom floor. A cursory examination by Knox found that the dead man had been shot through the heart. He also discerned that a railroad pass was clutched in Jones's right hand. As the Columbia *Record* noted, "The revolver with one chamber was found on a table in the room." The murder weapon proved to be a .45-caliber Colt revolver.

Furthermore, the police initially found the disconsolate father sitting upon the nearby bed. But he professed not to have seen the actual shooting. Apparently, no other eyewitnesses were to be found on the premises. Jones also maintained that he had not spoken with his son for several hours. Several neighbors, though, told police investigators that they had heard the two men engaging in a noisy argument about thirty minutes before the shooting. Accordingly, Detective Shorter decided to hold the father as a material witness. But no one believed the old man was the killer. Unfortunately, though, there were no other viable suspects during those early hours.

The following morning, one neighbor, Elijah Woodson, told Detective William T. Kelly that he had observed a young black girl departing the house minutes after the shooting. But investigators could not find any collaborating eyewitness. "All the other negroes [*sic*] who were questioned swore they did not see anyone leave the house," a reporter complained. Meanwhile, an anonymous informant told Chief of Police Fred S. Strickland that Miss Aileen Smith "knew something of the murder." Upon receiving that tip, she was picked up in front her home at 522 College Street. The arresting officer, Sergeant Knox, discovered that the pretty young woman was a "deaf-mute."

Chief Strickland was told that the suspect recently had completed training at the Cedar Springs Institute in Spartanburg, South Carolina. Unable to locate a proficient sign interpreter, seventeen-year-old Miss Smith was obliged to answer all queries in writing. But she was quite capable of lip-reading her interrogators' remarks. An impressed journalist declared, "She is very intelligent and seldom hesitated in answering each question made by the officers. Although a mere girl she writes in a very legible hand."

She readily admitted to having been involved romantically with Jones for the last four months. The girl was aware that his father strongly disapproved of this love affair. Smith had decided to visit Jones before he left for Richmond. Apparently, the elder Jones was in the back woodshed when Smith arrived. "She avowed that Jones had summoned her to his bedroom and became too amorous," the *Record* added. Brown also insisted that she had begun resisting his advances. Such resistance, however, drove him into a fierce rage. Amidst a violent physical struggle, she had procured the loaded revolver lying upon a dresser. Shooting at point-blank range "the bullet struck home with devastating results." After tossing the pistol aside, she promptly ran from the house.

Due to her voluntary confession, Miss Smith was charged with second-degree murder, in lieu of $1,000 bond. Chief Strickland told reporters that several prominent black businessmen had secured her quick release. They also arranged for the noted African American attorney, Nathaniel J. Frederick, to serve as legal counsel. No commentator could recall that a criminal defendant with her specific condition ever had been prosecuted within a South Carolina courtroom. The *Record* opined, "This case is highly unusual...and probably establishes a legal precedent in this state." Accordingly, her trial in Richland County General Sessions Court, convening on June 23, 1923, drew considerable public interest. Presiding over the trial was Circuit Court Judge J.P. Stoll. Throughout the trial a large crowd of spectators eagerly followed the proceedings.

With Everett Gaston interpreting, the defendant testified in sign from the witness box. She insisted that the deceased had been trying to choke her to death with his strong hands. Consequently, his intended victim had fired in self-defense. Of course, there were no eyewitnesses, including the grieving father, to refute her testimony.

After deliberating for twenty minutes, the all-white male jury rendered a "not guilty" verdict. Upon hearing the decision Charles Jones "collapsed in a state of apoplexy." But he staged a strong recovery in the emergency room at Good Samaritan Hospital. In marked contrast, the majority of spectators were delighted with the acquittal.

Two days after the trial Aileen Smith boarded a Seaboard Air Line Railway bound for Jacksonville, Florida., where she would be residing with an aunt. She intended to make a fresh start with her life. She clearly wanted to put this tragic episode in the past.

Catching Some Unexpected Characters

For many months the Columbia police were suspicious that illicit happenings were occurring within Cephas Neeley's home at 909 Walnut Street Although the African American man had no prior criminal record, some notorious characters were seen around his house. Consequently, on March 3, 1918, Detective Shovine S. Shorter and Officer William T. Kelly were conducting a surveillance on that building while parked in a Dodge roadster down the street. They had been tipped off that a white army deserter might appear.

About 7:00 p.m., they noticed a jaunty black man striding down the sidewalk "all dressed up and distinctly classy." Shorter recognized this dapper pedestrian as Thomas "Ginger" Cooper, a recently escaped convict from the Hampton Creek Work Camp. Apparently, he had reached Columbia "where he exchanged his prison garb for less conspicuous attire." Quite likely, he was staying with friends in the Wheeler Hill neighborhood, as well as again dabbling in bootlegging. The officers suspected that he was heading to Neeley's home to await an illicit liquor consignment.

The fugitive offered no resistance when the officers confronted him. Upon his person they found a pint whiskey flask, along with a .38-caliber pistol. By telephone in a nearby house, Kelly quietly arranged for some colleagues to convey the prisoner to the Columbia City Jail. The following morning Ginger would be sent back to the work camp. But he was not their primary quarry that evening.

They actually were after Private Earle Cherry of Flint, Michigan, who had deserted from Camp Jackson in late November 1918. Upon completing basic training he had been slated to accompany his infantry company to France. This doughboy, however, had no intention of participating in World War I. For over three months some local residents apparently had been abetting this desertion. For instance, he had procured suitable civilian attire upon the local black market. And he was spotted driving a tan Ford touring car down Lincoln Street. An informant told Officer Kelly that the deserter would be making an appearance at Neeley's house that night.

Around midnight Cherry finally drove up in his automobile. As the Columbia *Record* noted, "He speedily rounded the corner and was almost upon the officers in a flash." They quickly arrested the deserter before he could either resist or run. A reporter later quipped, "Private Cherry did not simply walk into a trap, but rode into one in a high-powered auto, thus adding a new version to an old saying." Within several hours he was reposing within the Camp Jackson Stockade.

The next morning Captain Fred S. Strickland led a police raid upon Neeley's place. Although they found a black drifter, Zeb Godwin, sleeping within a back bedroom, otherwise the house was vacant. One onlooker remarked that Godwin had been loitering around the neighborhood for several days. While not wanted for any specific crime, he was arrested for vagrancy. City Recorder Charles J. Kimball eventually sentenced him to one month on the county chain gang "for loafing in these times of high national activity." But Godwin professed to know nothing about Neeley's whereabouts.

Meanwhile the raiders thoroughly had searched the house. Within a storage room they located $700 worth of goods recently taken from a Southern Railways freight car. "These stolen articles consisted of 30 pairs of shoes, shirts and dresses, saws, bolted goods, window blinds, soap, with many sacks of meal and groceries," the *Record* revealed. They also recovered a "substantial number" of jute bags stolen from the Southern Cotton Oil Seed Company's warehouse. Strickland told journalists that Neeley had been operating a "veritable thieves' emporium" They confiscated three hundred bottles of contraband corn whiskey as well.

The police surmised that Neeley had been warned about the impending raid. Accordingly, he had fled the city for "parts unknown." But various of his associates eventually were tracked down. Furthermore, Shorter and Kelly had "bagged" two fugitives. In the process they also inadvertently helped to expose a major burglary ring.

A Most Resourceful and Nimble Fellow

On February 24, 1911, about 2:00 p.m., City Recorder James S. Verner was concluding a routine court docket. Among those consigned to the Richland County chain gang was twenty-five-year-old Larry Davis of 1912 Lady Street. He was to spend the next two months working upon the various county roadways. But the resourceful Davis had other plans. Despite the close proximity of a dozen police officers, he made a successful getaway by jumping through the nearest open window.

According to the Columbia *Record*, Davis was "a chronic loafer and boozer." He already had served several stints upon the chain gang for a variety of offenses. As a reporter stated, "He is a continual loafer, well-known around all the pool halls on Assembly Street." Apparently, Davis was a free spirit, as well as fond of the "sporting life." Like most young black southern men during that period he was forced to work mainly as an unskilled manual laborer.

Contrary to press accounts, though, Davis usually was employed gainfully. He performed odd jobs for various African American merchants along Washington Street. Moreover, he was the regular janitor of the Maceo Theater at 1316 Assembly Street. The *Record* once described that establishment as "a moving picture and vaudeville house for the colored people," owned by Arthur Johnson, a "colorful negro [*sic*] showman."

Davis also earned spending money by participating within the local bootlegging trade. He routinely conveyed whiskey to the bootleggers' various customers. Around 9:00 p.m. on February 23, Police Sergeant Perry W. Knox observed Davis strolling down Lincoln Street, carrying a large burlap sack. Three patrolmen, therefore, stopped him to make an inspection. Upon finding a dozen pint fruit jars full of whiskey, they transported him within the patrol wagon to the city jail on Main Street.

The next morning he was brought before City Recorder Verner, whose court convened upon the second floor of the Columbia City Jail. Davis was charged with transporting illegal liquor, as well as vagrancy. Unable to pay an eighty-dollar fine, he was sentenced to the chain gang. A reporter recalled, "He sat down sullenly. All show of innocence gone at the announcement of the penalty." A chain gang guard supervisor, Sergeant J. Calvin Clark, took charge of Davis and nine other prisoners. When the transport wagon failed to appear on schedule, Clark ordered them to sit on a wooden bench near the back door.

With the court adjourned, Verner and Police Chief W. Clinton Cathcart had walked into an adjoining room for coffee. Although a dozen police officers were on the scene, no one was paying much attention to the prisoners, and Clark was chatting with a friend downstairs. But no bystander had noticed that Davis was sitting next to an open window. Consequently, within a few seconds, Davis successfully had made his escape.

According to an eyewitness the other prisoners passively watched Davis climb out the window. He firmly grasped the sill with his hands, before kicking out from the outside wall. Davis successfully made a drop of twelve feet into an adjacent alley. A journalist noted, "He gracefully landed on his feet with no apparent hurt."

Meanwhile, a dozen employees of the neighboring Capital City Laundry observed his escape. The proprietor, John A. Young, assured pursuing officers that Davis had dodged through a vacant lot, bound for Assembly Street.

Not surprisingly, the fugitive became the object of an intense dragnet throughout the downtown. His various known hangouts around Lincoln and Pulaski Streets were raided. Several officers also looked for him at the Maceo Theater. But no tangible sighting of Davis occurred for three hours.

While driving down Washington Street at about 5:00 p.m., Chief Cathcart finally spotted the fugitive. He was observed running through Sydney Park toward the Congaree River. The swift Davis, however, easily outran several pursuers and stayed just beyond shooting range. He finally disappeared from view after running into a tree grove. Although the police kept looking for a week, Davis never was seen again around Columbia. Most observers assumed that he probably had caught a passing freight train. A rumor later circulated that he had gone to Louisville, Kentucky, for a fresh start.

City officials sadly agreed that iron bars should have been on that window. A year earlier another prisoner had made a similar effort through the same opening, but that luckless individual had broken his right foot during the attempt and was recaptured within several minutes. In any case, Davis's bold escape was a huge embarrassment to the city police. Chief Cathcart and his colleagues certainly were aware that countless individuals around town were telling many jokes at their expense.

Part III

This Escape Ended Quite Badly

About 10:00 a.m. on April 5, 1932, Charles Fitzgerald, the groundskeeper at Idlewood, a country estate, was making his mid-morning rounds. John C. Lott's sizeable property was situated along Garner's Ferry Road, approximately five miles from Columbia. Upon approaching the large fishing pond sitting within the middle of Idlewood, Fitzgerald was astounded to discover a corpse floating on the surface.

Four days earlier, during the noon lunch break, five African American convicts had escaped from a work detail performing repairs on a rural roadway near Killian. Two of the fugitives, Ernest Holmes and James Pough, were apprehended three hours later at the Sunset Fishing Club. Their capture occurred as they were preparing to shove a stolen rowboat into the Congaree River. A third escapee, John Shaw, was caught stealing meat from a farm smokehouse nearby to Hopkins. Sheriff T. Alex Heise of Richland County, however, admitted that the other runaways, Columbus Cheeks and James Henry "Hoss" Davis, narrowly had evaded capture outside of Eastover. They parted company after Hoss headed off to catch a passing freight train.

Meanwhile, thirty-five-year-old Cheeks planned to make his way into Columbia, where old Wheeler Hill associates likely would be providing him with shelter. Cheeks was serving five years for a series of downtown grocery store burglaries. While passing through one farmhouse he had purloined a pair of overalls hanging upon a clothesline, and a sympathetic black sharecropper had loaned him a hacksaw to file off his shackles. During the evening, however, an armed posse began pursuing Cheeks closely when their bloodhounds picked up his scent. But around midnight his trail suddenly went cold. The convict's whereabouts was unknown for the next three days.

Apparently, to elude his pursuers Cheeks had scaled the high brick wall surrounding Lott's property. He did not attempt to enter Idlewood through any of the gates, because those entrances were securely fastened. He subsequently ran down the long cobblestone roadway "leading to a body of clear water about three acres in size." Stocked with trout and other game fish this pond generally was five feet in depth. As the Columbia *Record* observed, "The desperate man likely stumbled into the pond in the darkness since those bloodhounds were pressing on his trail." Because the vestiges of those shackles had nullified his ability to swim, Cheeks died by drowning.

His corpse remained beneath the surface for the next seventy-two hours. After Lott was summoned he noticed that "the waters had washed the pants below his armpits and the prison uniform was clearly discernable as he drifted on...the peaceful pond." Lott and two helpers hauled the body back on to dry land.

An hour later Deputy Sheriff William H. Thompson and Coroner John A. Sargeant arrived to examine the corpse. Because the weather had been cool the body was in relatively good condition. The deceased certainly matched Cheeks's general physical description. The convict was known to possess a sizeable scar upon his right forearm. Upon discovering this mark, the investigators knew that they had found Cheeks. Coroner Sargeant estimated that he had been dead for over three days.

After no relatives came forward to claim the body, Sargeant arranged for him to be interred within an unmarked grave in Randolph Cemetery. At an official inquest the coroner's jury ruled that Cheeks died from accidental drowning.

In any case, only Hoss Davis remained at large. The general assumption around Richland County was that he had "successfully jumped a freight" and left the region. Two years later, though, he was arrested for armed robbery in Huntsville, Alabama. He ultimately was sentenced to serve ten years within the Alabama State Penitentiary. At least Hoss had fared better than his erstwhile associate, Columbus Cheeks.

Some Action in the Tenderloin

Various pedestrians walking down Lincoln Street early in the morning on March 15, 1911, were astounded to discover an unconscious white man, clad in his underwear, lying upon the sidewalk. After some prodding, William McIntyre, a bottle salesman from Goldsboro, North Carolina, began to recover his senses. McIntyre declined to explain the exact reason for being in such a predicament. But he did declare that his wallet and an expensive brown dress suit were missing. And the traveling salesman did admit to having spent the previous evening "on the town."

The Columbia *Record* recounted that forty-two-year-old McIntyre had made regular business trips to Columbia during the last several years. He had checked into the Columbia Hotel on Main Street the previous afternoon and eaten supper in the hotel dining room with several associates. Although a married man, he also desired some intimate female company that evening. One of his dinner companions suggested, therefore, that he should head for the 1200 block of Gates Street, Columbia's notorious "tenderloin section."

The Columbia City Directory of 1911 indicated that nine brothels were concentrated in that neighborhood, all within close proximity. And the female owners of these households were described as "madames." Although the majority was listed as "colored," two of these "disorderly houses" were run by white women. Flanking these dwellings were two legitimate African American businesses, namely a blacksmith shop and a tannery.

In any case, the salesman chose to patronize Madame Bessie Walker's house at 1213 Gates Street, where he proceeded to spend three hours with one of her "girls." About 11:30 p.m., Walker cordially offered her client a glass of quality whiskey. Apparently, though, she had "doped up" this drink with some unknown potion.

As a reporter noted, "Mr. McIntyre drank this whiskey and within a few minutes he knew nothing." The victim later claimed to possess "absolutely no knowledge" of his whereabouts during the next few hours.

Upon regaining his senses, McIntyre promptly reported the situation to the police. They had been awaiting a specific reason to take action against those bawdy households for several months. Consequently, at about 2:00 p.m., Lieutenant John R. Swearingen led a police raid upon Walker's place. But some tipster already had warned the "major domo of the house" about their impending arrival. Although the madame was gone, four of her employees were arrested. Moreover, several anonymous "loiterers" (customers) were detained as well.

Policemen also raided the other brothels along the block. Accordingly, at Queenie Marion's house they gained an unexpected "door prize." Police Sergeant Davis B. Sloan caught Henry "Savannah Kid" Jones climbing out through a rear window. They had been looking for this slick black grifter for many weeks on a variety of charges. At another dwelling officers also nabbed John "Dynamite" Tastley, a prime suspect in several recent armed robberies.

Meanwhile, an informant had told Officer Michael C. Turbeville that Walker was hiding out within Lizzie Williams's dwelling at 1000 Lady Street. The raiders caught Tilda Hampton pouring a gallon jug of corn whiskey down the kitchen sink. A search of the premises found Walker hiding under a large brass bed. And they encountered John Pierce, attired in a natty brown dress suit, sleeping soundly upon the mattress. Turbeville found ninety dollars in cash hidden within the bedsprings, along with a comparable amount upon the madame's person.

Not surprisingly, all persons caught at Williams's house were transported to the Columbia City Jail. Swearingen curtly dismissed Pierce's claim of having bought this new suit from a street vendor. The officers knew that the day laborer could not afford to purchase such expensive apparel. He eventually asserted that Walker had given him those garments as a gift. McIntyre later confirmed that Pierce had been attired in his stolen clothing.

By all accounts, seventeen persons were arrested during this police dragnet. City Recorder James S. Verner had a full docket the following afternoon. Walker was held over for trial on a charge of grand theft. Although the four "inmates of her disorderly house" each were fined forty dollars, they promptly paid those amounts "on the spot." Unable to pay her twenty-dollar fine for bootlegging, Tilda Hampton drew thirty days within the Richland County Jail. "Savannah Kid" Jones was transported to Charleston to face a safe-cracking warrant and "Dynamite" Tastley was looking forward to a long stretch in the South Carolina Penitentiary. While not charged with a specific crime, Pierce was convicted of vagrancy. Accordingly, he spent the next month working on the county chain gang.

Meanwhile, McIntyre already had departed quietly from the city. Doubtless, the salesman knew that he would be doing considerable explaining to his wife back in Goldsboro. But McIntyre had the satisfaction of knowing that he had recovered most of the money, as well as his expensive new suit.

The Prisoner Played the Piano in Jail

For two weeks in July 1921, a stylish, red-haired young woman, Miss Margaret Tipton, was a guest in the Jefferson Hotel at 1801 Main Street. From all appearances this attractive young "flapper" was quite affluent. Tipton told various acquaintances that she was a scion of a prominent family in Boston, Massachusetts. She further claimed that a female traveling companion had failed to meet her in Columbia. The pair was planning to travel southward to Key West, Florida. Initially, the hotel manager, Robert W. Carn, did not realize that he was dealing with a "classic check flasher."

By July 25, various downtown stores began complaining that Tipton's checks were worthless. She apparently possessed blank checks from several northern financial institutions, especially Chase Manhattan Bank. Despite smiling assurances, though, she failed to pay off any portion of her mounting hotel bill. Three days earlier she had "kited" a check after purchasing a pair of expensive shoes at Watson's Shoe Store. Accordingly, Herschel V. Murdaugh, the store manager, reported her to the police. Murdaugh discovered that other downtown merchants had made similar complaints.

Chief John W. Richardson noticed that Tipton matched the description of a young female wanted throughout the Carolinas for cashing fraudulent checks in a dozen cities. But that suspect had operated regularly with a female partner. In any case, Chief Detective Fred S. Strickland went to the Jefferson Hotel and arrested Tipton in the main dining room. As the Columbia *Record* observed, "She was dressed in tip-top style and made a very pretty prisoner." A search of her luggage revealed personal correspondence indicating that she recently had passed through numerous southern municipalities. Although Tipton admitted to having worked with a partner previously, "that person was not with her on this visit to Columbia." The two women evidently had parted company in Charlotte, North Carolina.

City Recorder Charles J. Kimball later set her bond at $1,200. When Tipton made no effort to pay that amount, she was lodged within the Columbia City Jail. A reporter duly noted, "She is one of the prettiest prisoners ever incarcerated in the city lockup." Since currently there were no other female inmates, Tipton began "taking life easy" within a second floor reception room. Interestingly, she spent considerable time playing upon a piano located nearby. Possessing a fine singing voice, she offered quality renditions of various popular songs, notably "Beautiful Dreamer," "After the Ball" and "Castle of Dreams." Not surprisingly, her musical offerings were heard by everyone throughout the building.

Police investigators eventually discovered that the prisoner had utilized numerous aliases during her travels. Chief Richardson was told by a law enforcement colleague in Memphis, Tennessee, that her real name was Ethel Clark. A native of Reading, Pennsylvania, she had broken all family ties several years earlier, preferring the life of an itinerant con artist. Moreover, this grifter had been arrested at least seven times, for a variety of charges. She cheerfully admitted that all this information was accurate. But the prisoner consistently refused to reveal her erstwhile partner's actual identity.

Meanwhile, she remained in jail for two months, awaiting trial within the Richland County General Sessions Court. She had retained a prominent local attorney, Clint T. Graydon, to be her legal counsel. Three days before the trial, scheduled for September 10, a dapper male stranger, Alexander Allison, suddenly arrived in the city. This mysterious benefactor, paying in cash, proceeded to liquidate all of her outstanding local debts. Accordingly, Circuit Judge J.K. Henry agreed to drop all charges against the defendant.

Obeying Chief Richardson's stern order, however, the pair promptly boarded an Atlantic Coast Line (ACL) passenger train bound for Miami, Florida. Various commentators generally agreed that this was a curious conclusion to a most unusual case. Furthermore, her musical performances certainly had enlivened "life in the jailhouse" for several weeks.

Serenading the Jailhouse

In September 1928, the residents of Lincoln Street generally considered forty-five-year-old Samuel Brown to be a dependable Southern Railways track maintenance worker. He was known, though, to become quite boisterous when drinking. Furthermore, Brown periodically exhibited a curious habit of clambering up to the roof of his house at 430 Lincoln Street, where he made considerable noise, much to his neighbors' annoyance. Interestingly, he resided directly behind the Richland County Jail.

By September 16, the county jail employees were losing patience with Brown's noisy antics. For the last three weeks he nightly had placed a ladder against the side of his house. After ascending his roof, Brown began waving a lantern toward the rear cell windows. According to County Jailer Henry W. Des Portes he was intent upon "carrying on a courtship" with several female inmates. Apparently, there was one woman that Brown particularly wanted to impress.

Quite often, his amorous comments were flavored liberally with strong profanity. He also loved to serenade those women with various popular songs. One guard complained to the Columbia *Record*, "The main problem is Brown can't sing a lick! His voice is terrible." Even the women Brown had been courting were becoming fed up with these goings-on. Unfortunately, Brown decided to resume his routine at sunrise on September 16. At that point, Des Portes finally decided to take action.

About 6:00 a.m., Brown already had climbed to the roof. As Des Portes told a reporter, "That guy was raising all sorts of racket today. He was cussing and cutting up something awful." All of that commotion had awakened the jailer and his wife, Ina, from a sound sleep. Throughout the jail all the guards and inmates were calling for Des Portes to silence their noisy neighbor. Consequently, he summoned Officers George Simpson and William E. Helms to arrest this public nuisance.

Initially, Brown ignored their order for him to get off the roof immediately. After he climbed down, though, they quickly concluded that the African American had been drinking. Brown vehemently insisted that he was planning to patch a roof leak that morning. Several days earlier he had gone up and finally spotted the hole amidst a rainstorm. Brown actually showed the officers his various work tools. But the policemen still did not accept Brown's lengthy explanation.

Within three hours he was appearing before City Recorder Charles J. Kimball. The prisoner was charged with disorderly conduct, public intoxication and willful interference of the jailhouse routine. Unable to pay the one hundred-dollar fine, Brown was sentenced to serve sixty days upon the Richland County chain gang. Someone remarked that he now had the "unique opportunity" of serenading his fellow prisoners while they worked on some county roadway.

Down into the Ground Went the Car

On February 5, 1927, at about 2:30 p.m., Thad W. Coleman, a Capital City Motor Company salesman, drove a new Ford roadster into a vacant lot beside the main showroom at 1235 Lady Street. He had parked the automobile nearby to the public sidewalk. While chatting with a prospective customer, Richard E. Halford, he noticed something peculiar: the vehicle's right front wheel was rising sharply into the air. As the two men stood watching the axle became quite visible. A bystander remarked that the roadster clearly was sinking into the ground. In fact, within several minutes the Ford had sunk approximately ten feet.

Not surprisingly, this singular sight quickly drew a crowd, including the company president, Campbell Courtney. Within an hour a tow vehicle had extricated the car from the sinkhole. Coleman and his associates certainly were relieved that the roadster had suffered only some minor body damage. Apparently, he had parked the car upon a long forgotten well.

An elderly onlooker, Young H. Vance, recalled that formerly the Swygert residence had been situated upon that spot. During the middle of the nineteenth century, John Swygert was a prominent Columbia businessman. Vance remembered that a spacious lawn, as well as a lovely flower garden, had surrounded the house. Furthermore, on February 17, 1865, Swygert's two-story brick edifice was among the few downtown dwellings to survive the infamous fiery conflagration ignited by Major General William T. Sherman's troops.

By 1918, that building had been remodeled and was Capital Motor's new headquarters. Meanwhile, the old wooden stable, still standing out back, was being utilized as a storage shed. But all traces of the lawn, including the garden, long since had disappeared. Several years earlier one of Swygert's grandsons had identified the site of an old well. In any case, Coleman unwittingly had discovered a second well.

Investigators later determined that this well possessed a circumference of ten feet, while the depth measured thirty feet. But no one knew exactly when the dry hole had been filled with dirt. Apparently, though, the surface soil had begun wearing thin as countless vehicles, varying in weight, drove over that space. For instance, three days earlier a large delivery truck had stood there for several hours. Upon driving the roadster on that same spot Coleman had delivered the final "coup de grace."

While watching the old well being refilled, Coroner J. Blakely Scott expressed relief that no one had been standing on that spot when the actual subsidence occurred. Otherwise, that hapless person probably would have experienced serious bodily injury. Accordingly, the ground was pushed down firmly this time to forestall any subsequent reoccurrence. Doubtless, the old well still is there, but now under a hard asphalt surface.

A Long Forgotten Burial Ground

In March 1933, Mrs. Raye C. Overton of 2714 Wheat Street made the decision to have a new cellar dug beneath her house. The widow hired Reuben Perry, an African American handyman, to undertake this excavation work. He brought along two helpers,

Samuel Williams and Charlie Kelly, to assist with the digging. On November 24, this trio was working away when they made a macabre discovery. While shoveling through some soil Kelly suddenly noticed that his shovel was bumping into a human skull, and his associates began finding other human bones.

While clearing away the soil, the workers subsequently located approximately seven complete human skeletons. Since Mrs. Overton was visiting her sister in Camden, Perry went next door to telephone the police. After listening to Perry's story with growing amazement, Grover C. Allen, the neighbor, went over to take a look. Within thirty minutes Chief of Police William H. Rawlinson, Sergeant Ernest E. Fellers and Coroner John A. Sargeant had reached the house. Allen willingly assured the police investigators that the three workers were good men.

Meanwhile, Sergeant Fellers had been inspecting the potential "crime scene." He noted that the respective skeletons were lying adjacent, as well as spaced about five feet apart. Allen also reckoned that the bones were located approximately six feet below the surface. Shreds of clothing and buttons were found amidst the human remains. Fellers concluded that he was viewing the vestiges of a long forgotten family cemetery. As the Columbia *Record* concluded, "Fragments of wood were found in each grave and these could be distinguished through the strata of the soil." Furthermore, his colleagues could not provide a better explanation. None of the observers were aware that any graveyard had existed upon that spot.

Although now within the Shandon section of Columbia, the property formerly was situated in the rural countryside beyond the city limits. During the last decades of the nineteenth century numerous small farms had existed in that locale. Apparently, the various remains initially had been placed within modest wooden caskets, which long since had fallen apart. And any grave markers had disappeared without a trace. The remnants of the clothing appeared to be of mid-nineteenth century vintage. Upon closer inspection Coroner Sargeant determined that two of the skeletons had been females. But he could not determine the specific racial origins of any of them. In essence, when Mrs. Overton's house was constructed there was no one around who remembered the old burial ground.

Meanwhile, the various skeletal remains were transferred to the custody of J. Whit McCormick, a local white undertaker. McCormick made sure that the skeletons were placed within solid new coffins. With little fanfare they were interred in unmarked graves amidst the "potters' field" section of the Elmwood Cemetery. Nevertheless, their exact identities remain an enduring mystery. In any case, Mrs. Overton's workmen eventually managed to excavate that cellar without further incident.

Whiskey and Blood Upon the Highway

In January 1923, many city residents were accustomed to watching twenty-eight-year-old Frederick Lee Suggs sitting behind the wheel of his fancy brown Maxwell coupe. He frequently was observed driving his "new high powered automobile" around the downtown streets. While known to be a capable salesman for a local shoe store, various observers still surmised about the means by which he could afford such an expensive automobile. Furthermore, Suggs always "sported" a stylish, expensive wardrobe. On February 28, however, such speculation ceased abruptly when Suggs was killed amidst a major car crash near Augusta, Georgia. Police investigators subsequently revealed that he also had been a key member of an interstate bootlegging ring. Suggs had died while making a "liquor run" between Augusta and Columbia.

Although a Horry County native, the victim had resided in Columbia for several years. He had been living with several male roommates within a house at 1314 Huger Street. During the day he worked as a salesman at the Saxon-Cullum Shoe Store on Main Street. Consequently, he had made a wide acquaintanceship among the city's "younger sporting crowd." Apparently, to underwrite his expensive tastes, Suggs had begun working with some bootleggers. Various friends began to note that he was making numerous "personal" trips to Georgia.

In any case, his fondness for fast driving proved to be his downfall. About 4:00 a.m., Suggs's car was speeding around a sharp curve along the Columbia-Augusta Highway when he suddenly lost control. A reporter for the Columbia *Record* wrote, "Prior to the crash he clearly was heading east at maximum auto speed." The vehicle probably "turned turtle" several times before crashing directly into a telegraph pole. Moreover, the driver was thrown nearly seventy feet from the wreckage. After the body was recovered, a medical examiner found that his skull was crushed and both of his legs had been fractured completely. One police investigator told reporters that "This was the most complete wreck that he had ever seen in his entire experience." While examining the victim's bloody clothing an officer noticed that his overcoat pocket bore the label, "F.S. Suggs, Columbia, S.C."

The Columbia *Record* mentioned that the police realized they were dealing with a major liquor smuggler. A reporter wrote, "Corn liquor trickled down the roadway for a distance of over ninety feet." In essence, they estimated that Suggs had been hauling approximately 175 glass pint fruit jars, each full of whiskey. Furthermore, they found glass fragments scattered in various directions all around the crash scene. Some shards were located a hundred feet from the wreckage. "Under the front seat, however, three half-gallon jars were found intact," it was added. An onlooker later maintained that a policeman drove off with this "evidence."

Sheriff T. Alex Heise of Richland County subsequently declared that Suggs's accident certainly was a critical setback for one local bootlegging outfit. Meanwhile, several friends traveled to Augusta to claim the body. Through the auspices of the Van Metre Funeral

Parlor, his remains were conveyed to Conway, South Carolina, for final interment. Of course, Columbians now knew that illicit "booze money" had financed his lavish lifestyle.

A Close Call for Miss Gray

By May 1926, Miss Wil Lou Gray of Columbia already was a well-known educator throughout South Carolina. She was serving with the South Carolina Department of Education as the supervisor of the program designed to eliminate adult illiteracy. Accordingly, Gray made frequent sojourns to explain publicly her work. Her frequent traveling companion was Miss Agnes McMaster, a Columbia teacher who strongly supported Gray's project. Apparently, all of these junkets had gone without incident. On May 19, the pair headed northward to Spartanburg, where Gray had a speaking engagement.

By all accounts, Gray's speech in Spartanburg was a "rousing success." After dining with friends, the two educators began the drive back to Columbia in Gray's tan Dodge roadster. They expected to be back in the city before nightfall. About 8:15 p.m., the automobile was making the approach to the Broad River Bridge in Lexington County. As the Columbia *Record* noted, "The approach to the bridge…winds about on the Dutch Fork side, like a mountain road." Always a careful driver, Gray was driving at moderate speed while approaching a sharp curve, situated several hundred yards from the bridge. At that point, she encountered an unexpected obstacle.

Sitting within the middle of the road were two automobiles. Eight men, "divided equally among white and colored" were standing upon the roadway, deep in conversation. A reporter wrote, "She was right on the party and rather than hit them swerved to the left." The car quickly plunged down an embankment, approximately thirty feet in length. "The machine headed toward the bottom of a ravine sweeping all in its path," the *Record* added. The vehicle ultimately struck a white oak which "caught the chassis in the front of the rear wheel just in time to send it crashing into a large log with more serious results."

Nevertheless, both women were trapped within the wreckage. And since the engine still was running there was the definite threat of the car catching fire. Of course, they loudly begged for those eight onlookers to render assistance. Although the four African Americans promptly responded, their white counterparts "tarried not." Instead, that quartet jumped into their vehicle and drove away "at full speed." Apparently, they did not want to be involved in any subsequent police investigation.

The black rescuers quickly extricated the victims from the wreckage. During the speedy descent, Gray had been thrown completely out of the driver's seat, while her companion was tossed under the steering wheel. McMaster suffered a broken right collarbone as well as a severely bruised left shoulder. Meanwhile, a deep laceration across her back required seventeen stitches. A lawman later declared the roadster to be "a total loss."

The four black benefactors willingly drove the injured women to Baptist Hospital in Columbia. Gray's personal physician, Dr. Jane Bruce Guignard, was summoned to supervise their medical treatment. Upon escorting the victims into the waiting room, however, the African Americans quietly departed the scene. A journalist wrote, "In the excitement the names of the negroes [*sic*] were not secured, much to the regret of both Miss McMaster and Miss Gray." Not surprisingly the police were curious about the identities of those white men "who went their way, leaving behind the injured parties."

Meanwhile, there was considerable speculation about the specific reason those eight men were standing upon the roadway. "No one thought to ask those negroes," a reporter complained. Sheriff T. Alex Heise of Richland County surmised that they were bootleggers, conducting an illegal liquor transaction. Consequently, all of them made sure their names remained unknown.

Following the accident, the South Carolina Highway Department promised to erect a wire fence around that dangerous curve. In any case, both women had recovered fully from their injuries within a few weeks. During the next four decades, therefore, Wil Lou Gray was able to pursue her eminent educational career. But that one evening in May 1926, her useful life almost came to an abrupt, violent end.

The Speeding Ice Truck Hit the Wagon

Following his usual routine, sixty-two-year-old Thomas H. Bowers arose at about 4:00 a.m. on September 11, 1926, to prepare for his weekly trip into Columbia. This well-known farmer resided along Garner's Ferry Road, approximately seven miles from the city. Every Saturday morning he delivered farm produce, especially butter and eggs, to his many residential customers. Upon completing the usual delivery route, he always sold the remainder of the inventory to the City Market, which stood at the intersection of Washington and Assembly Streets. Although possessing a truck, Bowers preferred to haul his products within an old farm wagon, drawn by a single workhorse. After reaching the city limits, the farmer usually proceeded down Millwood Road, then an unpaved rural lane.

As the farmer was driving into town, William "Sonny" Beacham and Jack Burnette were loading ice blocks into a delivery truck belonging to the Columbia Ice & Fuel Company. Around 5:00 a.m., these African Americans were to depart the plant, situated on Blanding Street, bound for Eastover. The company manager, J. Pryor Boyd, recalled that they had left on schedule.

Upon reaching Gervais Street, however, Beacham, the driver, decided to stop for breakfast at the Roundtree Lunch Room.

Apparently, both men were good friends with the female cook. At about 6:15 a.m. the proprietor, Warren A. Roundtree, reminded them that Boyd probably would be checking on their progress. Accordingly, they soon were speeding up Gervais toward Millwood. They realized that various customers in Eastover were sure to complain about their tardiness.

A pedestrian later declared that the truck had made a "mighty wide swing" on to Millwood. And Beacham was driving his vehicle on the left side of the road. While approaching the Epworth Orphanage at 6:45 a.m., the driver suddenly realized that Bowers's wagon was directly in his path. Unfortunately, though, Beacham was unable to avoid a collision. The noise from the head-on crash quickly drew the attention of virtually everyone upon the orphanage grounds.

Superintendent William D. Roberts observed that an unconscious Bowers was lying upon the front lawn over thirty feet from his thoroughly demolished wagon. Meanwhile, the horse was already dead. After being carried into the main building, Bowers passed away within fifteen minutes. An attending physician, Dr. G. Melton Roof, concluded that the victim had died from a major skull fracture. Another eyewitness, William E. De Loache, commented to a reporter that considerable debris, notably broken eggshells, was to be found all around the accident scene.

Conversely, the two occupants emerged unscathed from their overturned ice truck. Not surprisingly, Beacham was terrified to discover that the deceased was white. Consequently, he began running "at a brisk pace" down Hagood Street. But his companion, Burnette, remained behind to explain the situation to the police. Interestingly, Deputy Sheriff Thomas R. Davis subsequently found a quart fruit jar, full of corn whiskey, under the driver's seat. The runaway evidently did not wish to discuss either the accident or his connections with local bootleggers. One onlooker surmised that the pair periodically may have transported contraband whiskey as well.

An arrest warrant was issued for the missing driver. According to the Columbia *Record* Beacham's exact whereabouts were unknown for eight days. Sheriff T. Alex Heise of Richland County had decided that no charges would be filed against Burnette. By September 20, the fugitive voluntarily had surrendered to Heise at the Richland County Jail. Beacham explained that he had been "sorting out things" with relatives in Dorchester County. He was held under a charge of involuntary manslaughter.

Two months later, on November 10, he was sentenced to serve one year in prison, as well as pay a $200 fine. After an anonymous benefactor paid the fine, however, the jail sentence was suspended.

Meanwhile, Bowers was interred within a private family cemetery upon his farm. Apparently, many Richland County residents sincerely regretted his untimely demise. The *Record* also noted that major accidents between motor vehicles and wagons were becoming less commonplace around Columbia in 1926. That was because an increasing number of Columbians were moving out of the "horse and buggy era." Such a development was considered definite progress.

Mr. Gassoway's Curious Accident

During the afternoon of February 3, 1927, Henry C. Gassoway, the general superintendent of the Powell Paving Company in Winston-Salem, North Carolina, was concluding a major business trip. He had been inspecting his firm's various road construction projects in South Carolina. About 3:00 p.m., he was driving back in his enclosed Cadillac roadster to Columbia from Aiken County. Throughout this junket he had been staying at the Jefferson Hotel on Main Street. While traversing through Lexington County the businessman nearly experienced an unusual fatal accident.

About two miles from Lexington he was driving uphill at a moderate speed by the Casparris Rock Quarry, which had been abandoned for years. The old quarry crater, about ninety feet in depth, long since had filled up with accumulated ground water. Furthermore, this murky, stagnant pool stood approximately forty feet from the hard surface roadway. The driver was unaware that a sharp bend was awaiting him.

At that point, he encountered another automobile coming in the opposite direction "at full speed." The Columbia *Record* later reported, "Mr. Gassoway turned sharply to the left side of the road and…ran into a stretch of fresh earth, collected as road material." Meanwhile, his vehicle skidded directly into the quarry, where he was astounded that "calm green waters were rushing toward him." A police investigator later noted that skid marks indicated that the car "flipped over" a couple times before plunging into the pool. The Cadillac rapidly sank toward the bottom.

The driver unfortunately had left his right window open about six inches. Accordingly, the enclosed interior rapidly filled up with water. Upon reaching bottom, however, he managed to kick out the window in order to swim to the surface. After surfacing, though, Gassoway discovered that the nearest bank was thirty feet away. Being mid-winter those waters also were "numbingly cold." As a reporter noted, "The other car…had driven on, ignorant of Mr. Gassoway's danger."

Within five minutes, though, an open truck full of African American laborers was passing by, bound for Lexington. When this group observed the white man's predicament they promptly stopped to render assistance. A young man swam out to pull Gassoway toward shore. At that point, a curious event was occurring: "Mr. Gassoway's felt hat, lost somewhere in the journey…again rose to the surface and was rescued." Meanwhile, the truck driver had driven into Lexington to report the accident.

Gassoway was conveyed to Baptist Hospital in Columbia for emergency medical treatment. Apparently, though, he was present the next afternoon when the Cadillac was hauled to the surface. All of the observers agreed that the roadster was a total loss. Moreover, they agreed that a roadside barrier should be placed at that curve to preclude a similar accident. Not surprisingly, Gassoway wasted no time catching an Atlantic Coast Line (ACL) train, bound for Winston-Salem. He certainly had been in Columbia long enough.

Two Sports in Trouble

About 4:00 p.m. on November 14, 1923, Sheriff T. Alex Heise of Richland County received an angry telephone call from Frank Dunning, a Two Notch Road farmer. He declared that two young male strangers from Michigan were making "improper advances" toward his teenage daughter. Apparently, they had persuaded the teenager (left unnamed) to take several rides in their new Studebaker Special touring car. And one of them was coaxing her to go with them on a trip to Jacksonville, Florida. The sheriff also was informed that the fancy automobile was brown. Accordingly, the irate father was assured that these two "sports" would be arrested on sight.

Three hours later Rural Officer Albert Eleazer spotted the distinctive vehicle parked in front of a grocery store on Bluff Road. He promptly arrested the two men, thirty-two-year-old Edward J. Craft and twenty-four-year-old Bert Baly, both Detroit residents. They claimed to be "innocent tourists" passing through the city toward Florida. Although the pair denied any immoral intentions regarding the girl, they were hauled off to the Richland County Jail on Lincoln Street. After booking them, Heise decided to inspect their stylish vehicle. As the Columbia *Record* proclaimed, "Mr. Heise discovered these two 'sports' were driving one of the most unique touring cars ever seen around Columbia." The sheriff realized that two major interstate bootleggers were in custody.

The Studebaker carried eleven copper tanks with a collective carrying capacity of 150 gallons. "The rear trunk contained two large copper tanks with iron screw tops," it was added. Furthermore, a special heavy iron key was necessary to turn these screws. Eleazer further discovered five similar contraptions beneath the front seating. "Under the flooring from the rear wheels to the front seat there was found," a reporter added, "a long and wide iron trough." All of these containers provided the investigators "with the strong odor of whiskey." The *Record* further proclaimed, "The manner in which these tanks were arranged made this auto a virtual 'dreadnaught' in the field of transporting liquor."

Although the vehicle bore a Michigan license plate, within a strong box, the police found tags for five other states as well. They also found a road atlas featuring precise directions for all roadways running between Michigan and Florida. And there was a box full of straw wrappers, which customarily insulated the whiskey bottles.

The investigators managed to extract several tablespoons of liquid from within the nearly empty tanks. A journalist wrote, "Several officers and a newspaper man drew long breaths and all agreed it was mighty good brandy or rye whiskey." Someone then applied a lighted match to the liquid "which burned just like it contained alcohol." Federal Agent Peter J. Coleman guessed that the pair regularly hauled liquor northward from Florida. Doubtless, they had been making deliveries to various local customers.

Despite this evidence, though, the two men denied they were bootleggers. Craft admitted readily that he owned the automobile. As a Detroit real estate broker, Craft claimed that he annually made many business trips to Florida. He recently had bought this car from a client in Bradenton, Florida. He did admit, however, that a mechanic had warned him about all the Studebaker's unusual gadgetry. He kept insisting, "I don't have enough money to do such a risky business as bootlegging." Meanwhile, Blay professed to be Craft's employee, merely accompanying his boss on a routine sales trip. The police certainly noticed that Blay "added little to the discussion." Neither prisoner was inclined to provide a cogent reason "as to why they were driving around in a vehicle so equipped for hauling booze."

Ultimately, they were convicted in federal court in Charleston for the interstate transportation of illegal alcoholic beverages. They were sentenced to serve five years "at hard labor" within the Atlanta Federal Penitentiary. As was customary, Craft's Studebaker was confiscated and sold at public auction. Doubtless, both men regretted greatly that they ever had become interested in that "farmer's daughter." Consequently, her angry father had directed Sheriff Heise's unwelcome attention in their direction. They had learned the hard lesson that it was unwise to mix business with pleasure.

Certainly a Strange Theft

On February 9, 1920, the Reverend William H. Cross of Rock Hill, South Carolina, arrived in Columbia aboard a Southern Railways passenger train. Although only recently recovered from a bout of influenza, the redoubtable Southern Baptist evangelist was keen to hold to his annual Richland County revival mission. For a decade, every February, he held lively tent services, which always drew large audiences. During this sojourn, though, certain unknown parties decided to thwart Cross's best efforts.

Upon reaching town, Cross initially checked into the Jefferson Hotel on Main Street. He subsequently headed toward a vacant lot on Assembly Street. His chief assistant, William E. Cobb, had arrived two days earlier to make the preliminary arrangements for the upcoming nightly services. With several African American workmen they spent the afternoon erecting a large canvas tent, measuring forty feet in diameter, as well as in length. To hold this structure in place, they pounded ten solid wooden side poles into the ground. Cross recently had purchased this "spanking new" tent from the Cotton States Tent Company. Cross also had placed a wooden podium and portable altar within the tent. When the preacher and his helpers departed at about 5:00 p.m., their handiwork "shone spick and span in the waning afternoon sun." Cross did not believe that it was necessary to place a night watchman at the site.

The next morning the preacher received a stunning shock, which left him speechless. As the Columbia *Record* revealed, "The big tent had been torn down and was nowhere in sight." All of the poles were gone as well. The thieves even had stolen both the altar and pulpit. The distraught Cross promptly summoned his old friend, Sheriff John C. McCain of Richland County.

Not surprisingly, reports about this strange theft had circulated throughout the downtown. A journalist observed, "The stealing of this tent is one of the most unique crimes that ever has been reported to local police." Although a large crowd of curious spectators had gathered at the crime scene, no one admitted to witnessing the actual theft.

Sheriff McCain declared that the thieves certainly knew their business. For instance, they apparently had packaged the various tent sections within the proper boxes. They likely had deposited the stolen merchandise within a large truck. No observer, however, could explain logically their motivations for heisting the altar and pulpit.

Despite a subsequent police investigation no suspects ever were apprehended. McCain advised the upset preacher that the tent probably had been sold upon the regional black market. All of the equipment likely was to be found already within another southern state. Fortunately, though, Reverend Cross was invited to convene his nightly meetings at the Free Will Independent Baptist Church on Bluff Road. But Cross ruefully told friends that he still had to purchase a new tent for his subsequent outdoor revival services in other cities.

The Preacher Raised a Ruckus

About 7:00 p.m. on March 9, 1921, the weekly Sunday evening service was underway in the Apostle Holiness Church at 1507 Williams Street. At that point, Reverend Wilbur H. Wallace suddenly entered the sanctuary through a side door. Upon shoving aside an irate deacon, Wallace began addressing the startled congregation. As the Columbia *Record* reported, "He declared that the wrong doctrine was being expounded and it was his duty to stop the service." He then proceeded to exchange fisticuffs with the current pastor, the Reverend Will Sheets. During the subsequent melee a woman ran outside to summon the police.

By all accounts, Wallace possessed a considerable grudge against the church. He had been the Apostle Holiness's founding minister in 1910. Since he was not an ordained clergyman, for many years Wallace had worked as a fireman with the Atlantic Coast Line Railroad. He lived with his wife and three children in Arthur Town on Bluff Road. Using his own funds, Wallace had made the original down payment for the Williams Street lot upon which the church was built. He had caused great discord, though, among the congregation during World War I.

The outspoken preacher publicly had advised young African American men not to register for military conscription. He sarcastically had described the entire conflict as the "white folks' war." Not surprisingly, such sentiments were regarded as seditious by the political and military authorities in South Carolina. But Wallace steadfastly refused to retract those statements. Bowing to official pressure, in June 1918 the church council had voted to expel their controversial pastor.

Throughout the intervening years that expulsion had continued to rankle Wallace. He was incensed further when women were elected to serve as church officers. And Wallace deplored the fact that a couple female ministers had held revival services within this sanctuary. He publicly denounced those developments as "both unscriptural and an utter abomination to the Holy Ghost." All of these "sins" were reiterated during his "voluntary sermon" that evening.

Apparently, Wallace still possessed a few supporters at Apostle Holiness, because Archie Booker and two other men sided with him during the brawl. Meanwhile, Police Sergeant Perry W. Knox and Officer J. Walter Hits had reached the scene. After considerable uproar the policemen were able to restore order. Under arrest for disorderly conduct, Wallace was lodged within the Columbia City Jail.

The following morning the "jugged preacher" appeared before City Recorder Charles J. Kimball. Several angry congregants were present to provide "vigorous comment" against their erstwhile pastor. Upon hearing this testimony Kimball observed that Wallace "deliberately had chosen to get mixed up in matters with which he had no concern." He subsequently was sentenced either to pay a fifty-dollar fine or serve sixty days upon the county chain gang. The city recorder also recalled that Wallace usually was "an industrious, law-abiding fellow." Accordingly, he suspended the sentence, providing that Wallace made no other "spontaneous appearances" at Apostle Holiness.

The congregants accepted City Recorder Kimball's decision with relative equanimity and Wallace solemnly promised not to disrupt any future Apostle Holiness services. In fact, the preacher proudly announced that he was planning to start a new church in Arthur Town. Consequently, he had no desire to waste two months laboring upon the Richland County chain gang. And his old church could "go to the devil."

She Was No June Bride that Year

During the first decades of the twentieth century the Reverend Charles Jagger was famous throughout South Carolina. The

Columbia *Record* declared him to be "the venerable Negro missionary for poor, aged colored men." He also was the pastor of the Roberts Bottom Baptist Church on Lincoln Street. Although his "saintly qualities" had earned him the respect of all Columbians, his close friends also knew that Jagger possessed a fierce temper when provoked.

On June 23, 1911, at 6:00 p.m., the missionary's daughter Annabelle was scheduled to marry Jeremiah Williams within the family home at 1313 Oak Street. Not surprisingly, Reverend Jagger would be officiating over the nuptials. A sizeable number of guests had gathered for the wedding. As the ceremony was beginning, though, an uninvited "visitor," Alma Washington of Arthur Town arrived on the scene. An eyewitness recalled that her subsequent remarks "had the effect of lighting a rag in a straw pile." Washington emphatically announced that she already was Williams's fiancée. "She showed up at my house and claimed him straight away," Jagger later remarked to a reporter.

Washington told Jagger that the groom had been living with her in Arthur Town for five years. She had faithfully supported him by working as a laundress. For legal reasons, though, they finally decided to marry officially. Accordingly, she had given him two dollars to purchase a marriage license. As Jagger sourly added, "But he took the money to marry my daughter instead." The irate preacher promptly called off the festivities. He informed the guests, "There will be no wedding bells tonight, nor any other night at my home."

In any case, these tidings caused considerable uproar throughout the house. The bride went into hysterics upon realizing there would be no wedding. And her older sister, Selena Jagger Bodkin, physically assaulted Washington, thereby precipitating a general free-for-all. Within a few minutes the brawlers were fighting out on Oak Street. Amidst all the tumult, however, Williams made his escape out the back door. Soon the entire neighborhood was watching as Jagger's burly nephew, Pink Bindenbaugh, brandishing a wooden board, chased the runaway for several blocks down the street. But the fleet Williams ultimately outran his pursuer. He was last seen running down Gervais Street.

For the next several days the bride's irate male relatives were on the lookout for the errant groom. By June 26, Reverend Jagger was hearing rumors that Williams was plotting to elope with his daughter. Apparently, he was boasting about his intentions to some cronies in an Assembly Street pool hall. For the next three nights Jagger and his two sons sat upon his front porch, "each with a loaded shotgun in readiness." But Williams was not foolhardy enough to make an appearance.

Eventually, someone told Jagger that the "prospective Lothario" had left the city aboard a train bound for Montgomery, Alabama. Two of Alma Washington's brothers evidently were "hot on his trail" as well. Meanwhile, Annabelle was coming to realize that she would be a spinster for the foreseeable future. Consequently, she resumed working with her father on his respective missionary endeavors. Charles Jagger's final comment was, "All I can say is I'm thankful that this weasel didn't manage getting in among my family." Amen to that thought!

Part IV

Much Luckier Than He Knew

Late in the afternoon on December 8, 1921, William M. Gibbes Jr., the Palmetto National Bank's chief cashier, was dealing with some unforeseen paperwork. The banker was obliged, therefore, to telephone his wife, Minnie, advising her that he would be late for supper. By 6:45 p.m., however, he was walking briskly through the downtown toward his house at 1430 Washington Street. Upon reaching the nexus of Washington and Marion Streets, Gibbes realized that he was alone on a dark, lonely corner. Apparently, none of the gas street lamps were working. At that point, though, he only was one block from home. Meanwhile, three bandits were hiding behind a nearby tree.

Several seconds before receiving a sharp blow to the head, Gibbes later recalled hearing footsteps coming up from behind. Police investigators surmised that the assailants likely had used a blackjack. Prior to losing consciousness, Gibbes also recollected "some shadowy figures hovering above him." While the victim was sprawled on the sidewalk they thoroughly searched his pockets, thereby garnering a gold watch and a wallet. Gibbes estimated that the robbers had gained sixty dollars in cash. Although Gibbes's briefcase was opened, they found nothing of tangible value. Accordingly, numerous important banking documents subsequently were found scattered about for several blocks around the robbery scene.

Several minutes after the assault two pedestrians came upon Gibbes. Consequently, he was taken to Baptist Hospital for emergency medical treatment. Attending physicians were required to use much stitching to close "a nasty looking wound" upon the back of his skull. They also discerned that Gibbes was suffering from a serious concussion. He also had two broken ribs and body bruises upon his right side. Prior to departing, the bandits evidently had delivered some vicious kicks to their fallen victim.

Due to the banker's prominence in the city, Chief of Police John W. Richardson personally took charge of the investigation. The Columbia *Record* declared, "The police are making a rigorous investigation of this case, which is one of the boldest robberies staged in Columbia in years." After three days, though, Chief Detective Fred Strickland ruefully informed the press that they still had no definite suspects. "It's a sorry situation that a prominent man was assaulted and robbed," the *Record* complained, "at a time when people thronged the streets a short distance from the scene." And the crime had occurred "within a stone's throw from the city's financial district." Not surprisingly, most commentators assumed the culprits never would be known.

Following the arrest of three white hoodlums on September 25, 1922, the Columbia police announced that the Gibbes case was solved. Sitting within the Columbia City Jail were Andrew Roberts, Jesse Cooper and Collie S. Hinson. "This notorious threesome is quite well-known to law circles throughout the state," a reporter explained. They were under arrest for murdering C.R. Cannon, an African American taxi driver, during a holdup on Whaley Street in March 1922. According to one journalist that slaying was "among the coldest murders perpetuated hereabouts in many years." Furthermore, they were guilty of numerous other criminal offenses, including the Gibbes robbery.

By May 1923, the three desperadoes had been tried for Cannon's murder in Richland County General Sessions Court. Upon being found guilty, they each were sentenced to life terms within the South Carolina Penitentiary. In any case, they never were prosecuted for robbing William M. Gibbes Jr. But he did have the satisfaction of knowing his attackers' respective identities. Given their records of violence, he was fortunate they had not murdered him as well.

A Most Brazen Downtown Robbery

Among the more popular downtown restaurants in February 1928 was the Sanitary Café at 1345 Main Street. Numerous pedestrians stopped by during the early morning hours for coffee and doughnuts. Around 6:30 a.m. on February 20, two well-dressed young men were in the café for a sinister motive, namely to stage an armed holdup.

About 5:30 a.m., the morning waiter, Gus Baas, had unlocked the front door on schedule. But he noticed that the electric outdoor lights around the front doorway were out. Furthermore, he noted that a new green Buick roadster was parked across the street. Baas was intent, though, upon accomplishing his various routine chores, including the removal of the cash within the main register from the previous evening. He was expected to place those funds into the Wells-Fargo safe in the back office. Several hours later the café manager, Mike Lean, daily walked two blocks to deposit the money with the National Loan & Exchange Bank.

Anyway, that morning both Baas and Preston Ashford, the custodian, were busily arranging some new dining room furniture. Accordingly, an hour after opening up, Baas still had not placed the money in the safe. About 6:20 a.m., two dapper young white men sauntered into the Sanitary Café. Several other customers, including two policemen on beat patrol, already had come and gone. The pair ordered coffee and some toast. When Baas returned with these orders, he discovered that one of the men had drawn a .45-caliber Colt revolver upon Ashford. He curtly ordered the waiter to raise his hands as well.

Meanwhile, his partner vaulted over the counter to empty the register. The café manager later estimated that the bandits had procured $119 in cash. During his return leap the desperado accidentally knocked over a large glass jar full of peanuts.

Consequently, peanuts, as well as glass shards, were scattered all around the counter. The Columbia *Record* added, "When the register was completely rifled the two walked calmly out...into the street."

While departing through the front door they roughly shoved aside Ordell Barton, the deliveryman from Taylor's Bakery. He observed the pair drive away in the roadster "going at full throttle." Several pedestrians subsequently watched the automobile speeding along Main Street.

Interestingly, throughout the robbery an African American cook, Daniel W. Wood, was sleeping soundly upon a cot in an adjacent storeroom. He usually did not begin cooking breakfast until 7:00 a.m. Apparently, he heard none of the commotion, including the loud sound as the glass jar shattered on the floor.

Not surprisingly, news of the robbery quickly spread around the downtown. Although burglaries occurred frequently, everyone agreed that this was the first armed holdup of a Main Street business "in a considerable while." A follow-up police investigation was undertaken by City Detective Robert S. Broome and Sergeant J. Guignard Taylor. But these investigators made little headway with this case.

Various motorists had observed the getaway car moving swiftly across the Congaree River Bridge toward New Brookland. The police surmised that the desperadoes probably were bound for the Augusta Highway. Furthermore, they were believed to be out-of-state gangsters passing through the Carolinas.

The police ultimately announced that the culprits probably had left the area within a few hours. Two days later, moreover, the *Record* ran a news dispatch reporting that a strikingly similar robbery had occurred in Statesboro, Georgia. Quite likely, those bandits were "taking their act" westward. Such itinerant banditry increasingly became commonplace during the next several years, especially after the advent of the Great Depression.

The Son Spotted His Dad's Car

About 7:00 p.m. on March 5, 1932, William M. Shand Sr. of 1621 College Street was horrified to discover that his new Dodge coach automobile was missing from its usual parking spot. The attorney was planning a drive over to Gervais Street on an errand. The blue vehicle always was parked upon the street in front of Shand's spacious residence. Consequently he summoned by telephone his good friend, City Detective Leroy B. Medlin. They were discussing this apparent theft when William M. "Munro" Shand Jr. suddenly drove up in that car, now in a notably damaged condition.

Various commentators later remarked that during recent months several other automobiles in the neighborhood had been stolen. And Shand's stylish new coach certainly was a tempting prize. The Columbia *Record* noted, "The block is not well lighted and the thieves had no trouble...after they found the ignition switch in the main lock." Detective Merlin advised the despondent owner that the culprits probably had driven the vehicle from the city. Meanwhile, certain unforeseen events were occurring out in Eau Claire.

For the last two days, the younger Shand and Joseph Hammond had been visiting friends in Winnsboro, South Carolina. After a stopover in Eau Claire, they were driving along the Colonial Heights Road into the Columbia city limits. About the time these motorists were passing the Seaboard Railway trestle in Colonial Heights, Hammond noticed a wrecked blue car, lying sideways, in a grassy knoll. Shand promptly declared that they were viewing his father's new Dodge. Of course, he was unaware totally of the recent theft.

Apparently, the thieves had "come to grief" upon encountering a sharp curve. They probably were speeding down a hill when the curve appeared unexpectedly. Various bloodstains upon the front seat upholstery indicated that at least one of the desperadoes had been injured in the wreck. But the culprits long since had fled the crash scene. Indeed, an African American eyewitness, Tillman Bush, reported seeing, about forty minutes earlier, three white men running from the wreckage.

The Dodge car certainly had been damaged significantly during the accident. "The coach was smashed in on one side," a reporter related, "and several of the [window] panes were broken." Furthermore, when they first spotted the wreck the car's front lights still were burning. Not surprisingly, they were perplexed regarding the circumstances behind the Dodge ending up in Eau Claire.

With the help of several onlookers they "righted" the vehicle onto the roadway. Despite the body damage, Shand realized that he still could drive the car. Consequently, he headed for College Street, with Hammond following behind in his own auto. As may be expected, the elder Shand was delighted "by the return of his classy new machine." Of course, everyone present was astounded by the coincidence that Munro Shand had encountered the vehicle in the first place. And somewhere within the vicinity of Eau Claire three thieves were bemoaning their abortive car theft.

No Baseball for Columbia Fans

Throughout the initial three decades of the twentieth century, the Columbia Comers had been among the elite baseball teams within the old South Atlantic League. By 1929, though, the franchise was defunct, due to severe financial problems. Consequently, local baseball fans were deprived of their annual summer pastime. They were delighted, in early 1931, when a colorful baseball man, Bernard "Bernie" McCoy arrived in the city to establish a professional ball club in the fledgling Palmetto League. They were unaware, however, that McCoy soon would be facing serious legal difficulties.

McCoy was well known around the Carolinas as a resourceful baseball promoter. Earlier in his career, McCoy had been a player, as well as a manager, for various southern minor league franchises. Upon securing quarters at the Hotel Columbia at 1200 Main Street in January 1931, McCoy went to work organizing the Columbia Roosters. He told Mayor Lawrence P. Owens that three former Major league players, Tommy Leach, Al Bridwell and Rube Marquand, were among his "silent partners." Bridwell would be the field manager, while Leach busily scouted out prospective ballplayers.

McCoy blithely assured various civic leaders that he was holding talks with Barney Dreyfuss, the owner of the Pittsburgh Pirates. The Comers had been the primary farm club of that Major league franchise. Their erstwhile ballpark, constructed in 1927 nearby to the state fairground, was known as Dreyfuss Field. Not surprisingly, McCoy wanted his new team to play all home games within that facility. He told Mayor Owens that a rental deal with Dreyfuss shortly would be concluded.

On April 3, however, all of these plans suddenly evaporated when City Detective Shovine S. Shorter arrested McCoy within the Columbia Hotel's main lobby. McCoy was chatting with the hotel manager, Lawerence D. Barringer, as the detective made his approach. Numerous spectators were incredulous as they watched the prisoner departing in handcuffs. Reports quickly spread around the downtown that McCoy now was reposing in the Richland County Jail. While being led away McCoy had declared, "This is all a big mistake, that's all."

Eventually, Chief of Police William A. Rawlinson told reporters that McCoy was in custody under a federal warrant. In October 1930, McCoy allegedly had transported two teenage girls from Detroit, Michigan, to Memphis, Tennessee, "for immoral purposes." He was described as the ringleader of a major interstate "white slavery" operation. Someone recalled that McCoy once had been arrested in Wilmington, North Carolina, for smuggling liquor into the country from the West Indies. A reporter wrote in the Columbia *Record* that

McCoy had told a visitor, "There's nothing to this charge, just one big mixup that's come up." But U.S. Marshal Allen B. Kale was determined that the prisoner would not "talk his way out of jail."

Unable to pay the $5,000 bond, McCoy remained in confinement for one month. Several of his would-be visitors were told by jail officials that the prisoner "could not be seen by anyone except the federal people." Local gossips claimed that the glib entrepreneur nearly had succeeded in convincing a guard into helping him with an escape attempt. And McCoy's attorney, John Hughes Cooper, steadfastly refused publicly to comment about the case. Meanwhile, Mayor Owens was bemoaning to reporters that "the status of the ball club is now dangling in the air."

On May 10, U.S. Commissioner R. Beverly Sloan convened a hearing to consider McCoy's extradition to Michigan. He ultimately ruled that sufficient evidence existed to warrant such an action. But Cooper sought to forestall McCoy's immediate removal by securing a court injunction from Federal Judge J. Lyles Glenn. Instead, on May 14, Lyles signed the final extradition order. He was to be transported by train under the custody of U.S. Deputy Marshal Andrew W. Bobolesky.

Accordingly, the following morning Bobolesky and the prisoner headed to the Southern Railway Depot. The *Record* noted, "The usually genial Mr. McCoy was mute in comment about his case." Some months later, word out of Detroit was that McCoy would be spending the next five years within the Atlanta Federal Penitentiary. Of course, every Columbia fan already knew that no professional baseball would be played in the city during the foreseeable future.

Too Far to Turn Back

Around 6:30 a.m. on December 12, 1923, two African American fishermen, Joseph Butler and Nate Sanders, were walking along the banks of the Congaree River in Columbia. Both men were looking forward to a couple hours of fishing at their favorite spot, nearby to the Southern Railways trestle. Upon nearing their destination, though, the pair suddenly encountered a white man sprawled on the ground. Initially, they assumed that the man had fallen to his death from the trestle. After closer inspection they realized he was unconscious, as well as severely injured.

Throughout the previous evening James W. Newman had been drinking heavily with cronies in downtown Columbia. About 11:00 p.m., however, he had left them on Blossom Street, intent upon returning to his residence at 1022 Church Street. Nevertheless, Newman decided to seek out a bootlegger across the river in Cayce. Since no public bridge then spanned the Congaree at that spot, such a trip was tricky in 1923. Accordingly, any pedestrian invariably was forced to utilize the trestle when bound for Cayce. The safest method was to hitch a ride on a passing freight train, usually within the caboose. Furthermore, other lucky travelers were able to procure an available handcar. But Newman decided to cross that span on foot.

Apparently, Newman knew that a freight train crossed the trestle at 11:30 p.m. and another locomotive did not appear for another hour. Around midnight, therefore, Newman was strolling casually across the span toward his destination, blissfully ignorant that the last train had been delayed for an hour in Augusta, Georgia. Consequently, Newman was beyond that span's center when suddenly he heard the locomotive approaching.

At that point, the terrified pedestrian began running in the opposite direction. He quickly perceived, however, that the train was moving too fast. Moreover, the crew was unaware that Newman was in their path. Rather than experiencing a horrible death under the engine wheels, he decided to leap off the trestle into the river. After saying a brief prayer he jumped into the darkness hoping for the best.

Newman subsequently toppled seventy-five feet to bare ground, missing the water by several yards. In any case, he did not recall the actual impact. As the Columbia *Record* stated, "He was instantly rendered unconscious, with both legs being broken." Because no eyewitness had viewed Newman's desperate jump, he went undiscovered for over six hours. Providing that the fishermen would not have encountered him, the injured man may have remained there indefinitely and died from exposure.

Upon being transported to Columbia Hospital, attending physicians found the victim to be in poor condition. Newman remained within a deep coma until later that afternoon. Along with the fractured legs, he possessed serious "bruises and abrasions" all over his body. As a reporter noted, "The right side of his head has been especially bruised to a considerable degree." And the doctors also found that most of his teeth in the lower jaw were knocked out. The *Record* further observed, " Mr. Newman is resting as well as can be expected, considering his circumstances." Although he remained groggy, that evening the patient was able to converse with his wife, Hattie, and other family members.

By December 14, Newman's physicians were telling journalists that he was going to survive, despite his extensive injuries. But a full recovery was "still far in the future." Consequently, he was not able to resume his machinist job at the Granby Textile Mill for many months. Doubtless, in later years, Newman experienced other "nights on the town," but he probably avoided crossing the Southern Railways trestle.

A Hot Fight in the Old Town

During the last two weeks of July 1930 Columbia was experiencing a severe heat wave. The police certainly were aware that amidst such hot spells many persons developed surly tempers. About 10:00 p.m. on July 24, Chief of Police John R. Swearingen received a frantic telephone call that a "full-scale brawl" was occurring at the corner of Main and Taylor Streets. He already knew that a street dance was being held at that intersection. Consequently, Swearingen personally led the squad dispatched to contain this riot, which was spreading up Taylor Street.

By 1930, Camp Jackson was under the South Carolina National Guard's jurisdiction. Throughout the summer various other state national guard units annually conducted basic training exercises at that facility. Due to a chronic shortage of barracks space many out-of-state guardsmen were finding quarters in private homes around town. For instance, Corporal Adolph Bustas of the Oklahoma National Guard, an Osage Indian, was residing with George E. and Sally Harmon at 2501 Main Street. This trio, therefore, went together to the yearly American Legion street dance, being held in honor of the visiting guardsmen. The festivities were to take place within a temporary wooden pavilion erected at the junction of Main and Taylor. By all accounts, everything proceeded smoothly until a group of drunken Florida troopers appeared around 9:00 p.m. "They were very drunk and seemed intent to cause some trouble," the Columbia *Record* observed.

At that point, one of these troublemakers, Charles L. Lucas, spotted Bustas dancing with an unidentified white woman. Since he possessed a "swarthy complexion" Lucas incorrectly concluded that Bustas was an African American. Not surprisingly, Lucas was enraged by this perceived breach of southern racial etiquette. He challenged the Native American to fisticuffs, but several onlookers hustled Lucas outside the pavilion. Unfortunately, he stood on the street "hurling racial slurs at Bustas." Apparently, he did not care that Bustas was a tall, burly man. A reporter later stated, "Finally Bustas came out, intent upon exterminating one Florida militiaman, unless he got a full apology from him."

Meanwhile, City Detective Walter T. Scott stepped between the two angry men. After several minutes of tense conversation, Bustas agreed to depart the vicinity. But he also declared that Scott appeared to be siding with the Floridian. Within five minutes, though, Bustas

108

had reappeared "in order to settle accounts with Lucas, who was still present." After Scott ordered the Osage "to go home and take a nap," Bustas punched him "squarely upon the jaw."

As the *Record* added, "Mr. And Mrs. G.E. Harmon attempted the ever-dangerous roles of peacemakers, with the proverbial reward." Upon exchanging verbal insults, Sally Harmon allegedly struck the detective with a china plate. And Scott's problems increased when "several friends of the Indian answered his war-hoop and charged the lone detective." Correspondingly, a fierce melee had "erupted" between the national guardsmen from Florida and Oklahoma. Amidst the free-for-all Bustas managed to find his primary antagonist, Lucas. After punching him several times, Bustas "smashed a bottle over his head."

With the riot intensifying, several other policemen appeared "to bolster the law and order army." A reporter declared, "Oklahoma soldiers, visiting citizens, Legionaries [American], and passerbys became participants in the fight...Bricks and bottles sailed through the air, and several pistols were drawn, but no shots were fired." The fighting also spread down the adjacent city block along Taylor Street.

Once Chief Swearingen and his squad of his twenty officers arrived upon the scene, the entire situation changed. They disrupted the brawling by forming a "flying wedge along the entire battlefront." Using billy clubs they proceeded to batter into submission the more recalcitrant rioters. At least twenty-five persons were arrested on various charges, mostly disorderly conduct. Moreover, some participants, including Scott and Lucas, went to Baptist Hospital for medical treatment.

City Recorder Heyward Brockington faced a heavy docket the following morning. He found Bustas guilty of disorderly conduct and resisting arrest. Brockington sentenced him either to pay a one-hundred-dollar fine or serve two months within the Richland County Jail. Subsequently, a journalist learned that several anonymous benefactors had paid that fine. Found guilty of disorderly conduct, Sally Harmon was sentenced to serve a month in the Columbia City Jail. But Brockington later agreed to suspend that sentence.

Charles L. Lucas, the initial troublemaker, was convicted of public drunkenness, as well as disorderly conduct. Recorder Brockington, however, agreed to turn him over to the Camp Jackson authorities for unspecified "military discipline." Another rioter facing Brockington was William Melwood, an Oklahoma soldier, "whose fiery red hair probably explains his entrance into the fray." Unable to pay a fifty-dollar fine, Melwood spent thirty days in the county jail. An inadvertent combatant, Charles W. Taylor of 1109 Gates Street, was exonerated of any wrongdoing. He had been walking peacefully up Main Street when "three or four men suddenly attacked him."

One week following the disorder the training course had concluded at Camp Jackson. Doubtless, Adolph Bustas wasted little time in heading back to Oklahoma. Furthermore, many national guardsmen in Florida and Oklahoma soon were explaining to their families the reason they possessed so many cuts and bruises.

A Most Peculiar Habit

On September 28, 1934, two Columbia residents, Samuel A. Devereux and Andrew Jacobs, were fishing in a pond adjacent to Lakeview Road, approximately seven miles beyond the city limits. About 8:00 p.m., they suddenly heard a loud gunshot emanating from a short distance away. Within a few minutes they found a well-dressed white man lying next to the roadway with a pistol beside him. He clearly was suffering from a major bullet wound within his upper chest. He refused to disclose to his benefactors the precise circumstances behind the shooting. He sullenly remarked, "If you were in as much pain as I am, you wouldn't want to talk either." Upon perusing the victim's wallet, though,

Jacobs discovered that he was thirty-five-year-old Andrew W. Nicholson of Columbia. And Nicholson's brown Dodge coupe was parked on a nearby side lane.

By all accounts, he had been residing with his aged mother, Mrs Delia A. Nicholson, at the Jefferson Hotel on Main Street for the last four years. Apparently, during the "Roaring Twenties" he was a prosperous stockbroker in Charleston. But the Great Stock Crash in October 1929 effectively had wiped out his livelihood. The Nicholsons subsequently moved to Columbia in 1931. Mrs. Nicholson's income from a trust fund paid for their quarters at the Jefferson. While investigating the shooting the police learned about Nicholson's "peculiar nightly ritual."

Prior to falling into "genteel poverty," Nicholson had been a sportsman, especially fond of duck hunting. Although he had abandoned that pastime, he still owned an Airedale pointer dog. Virtually every evening he drove the dog out to Lakeview Drive for training exercises within a pasture. During these trips he always carried a loaded .45-caliber Colt revolver. The Columbia *Record* further explained, "When the dog went into point [position] he would fire his pistol into the air." Accordingly, after hearing the gunshot, the Airedale terrier rushed off at full speed, returning only when Nicholson blew a dog whistle. Not surprisingly, many local residents had noticed him performing this nightly ritual. Someone recalled that Nicholson usually placed the pistol under his waistline belt while striding about amidst those sessions.

After discovering the victim, Devereux drove to a nearby grocery store and telephoned the police. Deputy Sheriff Wade H. Rawlinson of Richland County arranged for an ambulance to transport Nicholson to Baptist Hospital. Despite emergency surgery, however, the patient passed away about midnight. The bullet had extensively damaged too many vital organs, notably the spleen. Meanwhile, the Airedale apparently had gone missing from the scene.

Initially, Coroner John A. Sargeant believed that he had committed suicide, due to anxiety about his uncertain finances. Such incidents were common throughout that decade of severe economic crisis. But the coroner changed his opinion after conversing with Nicholson's mother. Consequently, Sargeant decided that the victim probably had stumbled, thereby accidentally causing the revolver to discharge. That conclusion was sustained officially after a coroner's inquest.

Interestingly, while police investigators were interviewing Mrs. Nicholson, the Jefferson's front doorman reported that the missing dog "had come home searching for his lost master." Despite the odds, that resourceful Airedale terrier had pointed in the right direction. Unfortunately, though, Nicholson was not present to reward him for this gallant effort.

A Fatal Gun Demonstration

A popular sportsman around Columbia was Charles S. Little, the manager of the Richland Dairy Company, a firm known for manufacturing quality ice cream. He generally spent most of his leisure time either hunting or fishing. During his army service in World War I, Little had developed a notable proficiency with firearms. About 8:30 p.m. on June 12, 1932, he arrived at the company plant on North Main Street in his Essex roadster. Leaning upon the front seat was a new .15-gauge double-barreled shotgun. After work he was intending to hunt small game on his cousin's Lexington County farm.

Several minutes after his arrival, an employee noticed the shotgun. Little happily agreed to show off his weapon, and he demonstrated to his co-workers the complete military manual of arms drill. Little declined, though, to provide a shooting exhibition within the vacant lot behind the plant. He definitely remarked to someone that the shotgun was not loaded. As the Columbia *Record* noted, "He was setting the gun down, at the same time...

joking loudly about his hunting prowess, when the firearm was discharged." Apparently, he had slammed the gun too hard to the concrete floor. Little also had forgotten that his firearm actually was loaded, with a shell in each barrel.

In essence, Little was shot directly with a full load of buckshot. The first barrel discharged numerous pellets that penetrated into his right side, just below the rib cage. "The charge from the second barrel seared completely through his right leg," a reporter added. Police investigators later surmised that the powerful percussion from the initial discharge had induced the second explosion.

Initially, the various onlookers thought that the victim was joking when he loudly declaimed, "Oh dear Lord, I'm shot!" But Clyde W. Cottrell quickly observed that blood was flowing profusely from a gaping chest wound. Upon staggering several feet, Little fell senseless to the floor, never again regaining consciousness. All of the employees agreed that their boss appeared to be mortally wounded.

Two of his personal friends, Cottrell and G. Wilson Owens, carefully placed the dying man in the back seat of the roadster for the ride to Baptist Hospital. He died two hours later during emergency surgery. Since the shooting clearly was accidental, Coroner John A. McCain of Richland County decided that no official inquest would be necessary. The following morning the body was transported to Charlotte, North Carolina, for burial.

Meanwhile, Little's death was met with deep regret throughout the city. During his thirteen years of residence he had become a popular figure, especially within sporting circles. Moreover, many observers were incredulous that this skillful sportsman had fallen victim to such a careless accident. He apparently had forgotten that the gun was loaded. Unfortunately, though, with such mistakes usually there are no second chances.

A Most Happy Holiday Season

Around the downtown of Columbia, Garrison Langston of 1145 Lincoln Street was considered a "poor soul." Throughout 1931 this unskilled African American laborer had been surviving by performing odd jobs for various Washington Street merchants. Langston was telling friends that he would be returning to his native Fairfield County by spring. Not surprisingly, he was feeling little "good cheer" as Christmas approached that year. About 6:00 p.m. on December 21, Langston was trudging along the 1700 block of Main Street when he suddenly spotted a brown leather wallet lying upon the sidewalk. Retrieving this object allowed him to enjoy a "kingly Christmas celebration," because he also found $600 in cash.

Several minutes before Langston's discovery, Walter H. Hawkins, the owner of Hawkins Women's' Wear Shoppe, had locked up his store at 1714 Main Street and met his wife, Eunice, outside on the sidewalk. Subsequently, while climbing into his Dodge sedan, the merchant unknowingly had dropped his billfold. Several blocks away, when Mrs. Hawkins asked to borrow ten dollars for some shopping, he discovered that his wallet was missing. A reporter added, "Upon missing that item he quickly returned to the spot where he may have dropped it, but the wallet was already gone." Nevertheless, Hawkins was not too worried, since the wallet contained an identification card, stating his name and address. During the next two days, though, no "Good Samaritan" came forward with either the wallet or money. Consequently, he reported this major loss to the Columbia police.

Although later maintaining that he had asked several pedestrians whether they knew the owner, Langston soon decided to appropriate the money. He certainly made no serious effort to contact Hawkins over the next few weeks. Instead, various police officers were hearing reports around Lincoln Street that Langston was "flashing a big roll of greenbacks and spending it lavishly." For instance, he had paid fifty dollars in cash for a Ford coupe, while assembling an expensive new wardrobe as well. Local gossips also claimed that he had "spent a princely sum for holiday revelry." Another tipster told Police Sergeant J. Walter Hite that Langston had lost seventy dollars during a poker game in an Assembly Street poolroom. Hite told his associates that he probably knew the source of Langston's prosperity.

Suspecting that he was spending Hawkins's money, on January 6, 1932, Sergeant Hite confronted Langston on Lady Street. He had noticed that the dapper Langston was attired in an expensive new brown flannel suit. An inspection of his person produced a roll of seventy-five dollars in cash. The sergeant curtly dismissed Langston's claim that recently he had come into an inheritance. Moreover, Hite did not believe that the new clothing was a holiday gift from a female admirer.

Meanwhile, a search of Langston's apartment turned up Hawkins's wallet. Confronted with this discovery, Langston ruefully confessed to appropriating the cash. He was confined within the Columbia City Jail. Moreover, City Recorder Heyward Brockington ordered him to be held for petty larceny. At Hite's insistence he also was charged with vagrancy. Of course, Hawkins regained what was left of the money. By March 15, Langston had gone to trial in Richland County General Sessions Court.

Subsequently, while serving two years on the state chain gang, at least Langston could recall fondly those good times amidst the Christmas of 1931.

Too Much Noise from the Radio

During the evening of May 15, 1933, a mixed social gathering of young African Americans was underway at 2110 Pine Street. After consuming much food and drink, including corn whiskey, several of the women wanted some dancing. Unfortunately, though, twenty-three-year-old Albert "Kid Chocolate" Brown, their host, owned neither a phonograph nor radio. Accordingly, he proposed that they relocate the party to his family's house at 2200 Calhoun Street. He knew that his father, Emmanuel Brown, recently had purchased a new RCA radio. Brown and thirty friends, therefore, began walking toward Calhoun Street.

The older Brown, at fifty-five years, was a longtime employee of the Oliver Motor Company on Main Street, as well as an active member of Second Calvary Baptist Church. But his son, Albert, was known "to run with a fast sporting crowd." Furthermore, he was well known around Columbia as a natty dresser. He did earn a steady income, though, by working as a house painter. His nickname was due to a notable physical resemblance to Kid Chocolate, a popular Afro-Cuban featherweight boxer. Various relatives later told police investigators that "much bad blood" had existed between father and son for several years.

In any case, this boisterous crowd reached their destination around 9:00 p.m. Despite the strident protests of his mother, Mrs. Carolina Brown, Albert "turned on the radio to full blast." Within several minutes Kid Chocolate and his friends were dancing throughout the house. Not surprisingly, various households throughout the neighborhood soon were complaining about the racket. They did not appreciate being serenaded with musical renditions performed by Cab Calloway's orchestra.

About 10:00 p.m., Kid Chocolate and several friends were lounging on the front porch, sipping corn whiskey from a pint fruit jar, when his father finally appeared. He had been attending a lodge meeting at the Masonic Temple on Washington Street. Brown was furious that this noisy party was being held without his permission. He roundly denounced both the drinking and dancing occurring within his residence. He vowed to disperse the celebrants with a loaded .12-gauge shotgun.

Amidst their ensuing noisy quarrel, father and son began a shoving match. According to several onlookers the elder man had started swinging a large wooden board at his son. Meanwhile, Jasper Lowery had tossed a brick to Albert, which he promptly smashed over his father's head. An unconscious Emmanuel Brown toppled over the porch rail with a fractured skull. The son later maintained that he had acted in self-defense.

Several minutes later, five police officers finally arrived in response to angry telephone calls made by neighbors to Chief of Police William A. Rawlinson, complaining about the rowdy party. But Kid Chocolate already had fled the scene. He quietly surrendered the following morning, to City Detective Perry W. Knox, during a pre-arranged meeting within a cousin's house on Washington Street. Before dispersing the revelers, the police raiders had detained several of them as material witnesses to the assault.

Meanwhile, the unconscious father was transported to Good Samaritan Hospital for emergency medical treatment. Never regaining consciousness, the victim finally died at about 2:00 p.m. the next afternoon. Already lodged within the Columbia City Jail, Albert Brown now was facing a charge of second-degree murder. Although Jasper Lowery initially had been booked as an accessory to the crime, he never faced prosecution.

Albert Brown was ultimately tried for voluntary manslaughter in Richland County General Sessions Court. On June 6, 1933, Kid Chocolate was sentenced to serve three years in the South Carolina Penitentiary. But he probably spent most of that sentence upon a chain gang, laboring on some local roadway.

When reporting the case, the Columbia *Record* observed that the loud radio noise had been the original source of the trouble. Although similar incidents had occurred repeatedly around the city, no other episode had ended so violently. One commentator had remarked that such lively jazz was "too frantic for some folks to handle." And younger Columbians appeared to adore that music "beyond all reason." The reporter expressed amazement that such tragedies did not occur more often.

The Food Tasted Somewhat Peculiar

Throughout the summer of 1931, Will Mixon of 1215 Gates Street had been complaining about his health. By August 5, he was bedridden with a mysterious stomach ailment. Consequently, a neighbor, Lizzie Roberts, had begun attending to the invalid's daily needs, including the cooking of his meals. But Mixon eventually developed grave doubts about her motives.

Prior to this illness, he regularly had worked as a track maintenance worker with the Atlantic Coast Line Railroad. Various neighbors recalled that he usually enjoyed robust health. The local gossip circulating about the neighborhood was Roberts had taken out a life insurance policy on Mixon with Pilgrim Health & Life Insurance. Since December 1929 she had handled all of the regular premium payments. As the sole beneficiary Roberts would be paid $375 upon his death. Doubtless, this fact had raised Mixon's suspicions about his benefactor.

Lizzie Roberts certainly was a notorious character around Columbia. Although she usually was employed as a domestic worker, Roberts had other sources of income. She had been arrested several times for bootlegging. Furthermore, in February 1928, she was suspected of fatally poisoning her fiancé, John Henry Mims. After his demise she had collected $250 from the Standard Life Insurance Company. While most observers suspected foul play, police investigators were unable to gain conclusive proof. "Lack of tangible evidence caused that case to be dropped," the Columbia *Record* added. Dixon probably had heard the allegations about Sims's untimely passing.

About 5:00 p.m. on August 6, Roberts's best friend, Mamie Collins, went to Dixon's house with a "hot supper." While partaking he began suspecting "there was something peculiar about his dinner." As Dixon chewed upon a biscuit he "suddenly noticed a greenish spot on the plate and the discolor of the collards." Accordingly, he dispatched a friend, Elijah Woodbine, to bring over Isaac S. Leery Jr., a respected African American entrepreneur in Columbia. After analyzing those morsels, Leery decided to summon the police, because his suspicions were that "the food was laced with copper and arsenic."

Within thirty minutes City Detective Rowland McCallister had arrived at Dixon's house. The detective previously had been involved in the investigation of Mims's suspicious death. McCallister believed firmly that Roberts had "gotten away with murder." He agreed with Leery that Dixon's situation was reminiscent of that earlier case.

Although Detective McCallister promptly headed next door to confront Roberts, he found that her place was vacant. He was planning to depart when Collins unexpectedly walked through the back door. During a subsequent grilling she readily confirmed that Roberts had been poisoning the invalid for several weeks. Collins vehemently denied, however, that she had assisted in this nefarious scheme. Several hours later Roberts was apprehended while strolling down Washington Street.

Not surprisingly, the two women told conflicting accounts about the recent sequence of events. City Recorder Heyward Brockington eventually ordered that Roberts be held for attempted murder, while Collins was charged as her accessory. This "precious pair" spent the next two months within the Richland County Jail. During that interlude, though, Collins agreed to testify against her erstwhile friend. Circuit Judge William H. Townsend sentenced Roberts to three years confinement within the South Carolina Penitentiary. But the charge against Collins was dropped. Apparently, she resumed working around town as a domestic servant for prominent white households.

Upon gaining some proper food, Dixon rapidly regained his health. He was well enough to offer vigorous testimony against

Roberts at her trial. And he resumed working for the Atlantic Coast Line. Later that year he decided to relocate to Allendale, South Carolina, his old hometown. Meanwhile, Dixon certainly named another beneficiary for his life insurance policy. And he was in no hurry to have that lucky individual claim that money.

He Was All Burned Up

By January 1934, numerous African American proprietors operating in the vicinity of Washington and Lady Streets were complaining that their businesses had experienced frequent burglaries. Because of the high unemployment brought on by the Great Depression, many poor Columbians were resorting to crime. For instance, J. Parker Long's café at 1001 Lady Street had been robbed five times since September 1933. As a precaution, therefore, he hired forty-five-year-old John Floyd "to spend his nights in the place in the hope of apprehending the robbers." Armed with a loaded .32-caliber pistol, Floyd usually spent the long hours lounging upon an easy chair in Long's back office. The owner was confident that the burly watchman could handle the situation.

For the last three months, however, Floyd had been in a "grieving state" since his wife, Bessie, had died of lockjaw. The widower told friends that he was "mighty lonely" in his apartment at 1808 Washington Street. And after losing his job at the Jefferson Hotel, Floyd was earning money by performing manual labor for various downtown merchants. Accordingly, he eagerly accepted Long's job offer. But various neighbors also were noticing that Floyd was exhibiting peculiar behavior.

About 11:00 p.m. on January 5, Floyd had locked the café doors and began his nightly vigil. An hour later Rosa Samuels, who resided in a neighboring apartment, suddenly heard horrifying screams emanating from the eatery. Samuels and several pedestrians looked through the front window "only to observe Floyd in flames." Meanwhile, Officer John E. Taylor reached the scene after hearing the loud commotion. The patrolman had been walking his regular beat along Lady Street.

Upon knocking down the front door, everyone rushed to the fallen, unconscious victim. They quickly noted that his body had suffered extensive burns. A neighboring restaurant proprietor, Richard Carroll, volunteered to transport him to the Good Samaritan Hospital. Officer Taylor and several bystanders carried Floyd out to Carroll's automobile. After suffering four hours of acute pain, he finally died at 4:00 a.m.

Coroner John A. Sargeant commenced his official investigation later that morning. Several of Floyd's friends told him that the deceased lately had been exhibiting some erratic behavior. He had developed the "curious habit of putting his pipe…still filled with burning tobacco, into his coat pocket." Accordingly, his clothing had ignited on several occasions. But he always had managed to douse water upon the burning garments in time.

A black undertaker, Thomas H. Pinckney, suggested that this latest episode had occurred while Floyd was dozing in the easy chair. The victim apparently had made a desperate dash to the front door after realizing that he was burning up. While going through Floyd's jacket a hospital attendant had found his pipe within the right pocket. And charred tobacco was evident in the bowl.

At that point, Coroner Sargeant decided that no inquest would be necessary. Due to the disfiguring burn wounds, Pinckney placed the corpse within a closed wooden coffin. Although not a regular member, Floyd's funeral was held at First Calvary Baptist Church on Richland Street. He was interred next to his wife's grave at Randolph Cemetery. When discussing the case all observers agreed that Floyd's death was among the most bizarre that they ever had encountered.

Welcoming Rudy Vallee to Columbia

Anyone familiar with the Seaboard Air Line Station on Gervais Street probably knew that the Orange Blossom Special arrived daily at 9:00 a.m. This locomotive traveled regularly between New York City and Miami Beach, Florida. On February 5, 1933, an unusually large crowd had congregated at the platform to await the train's arrival. They were planning to greet the popular American singer, Rudy Vallee. Everyone was thrilled with the prospect of meeting "the blue-eyed, fair-haired crooner."

According to the Columbia *Record* a railroad employee in Raleigh, North Carolina, had wired Carson N. English, a local Seaboard official, that Vallee was aboard the Orange Blossom Special. Word of his impending arrival quickly spread throughout the downtown. Accompanying the crooner were his backup musicians, the Connecticut Yankee Orchestra. They were about to commence an extensive southern tour of six weeks. In fact, Vallee was slated to appear at the Columbia Township Auditorium on February 26.

At that point, Vallee was at the height of his notable singing career. Since 1928, he had been hosting the *Fleischman's Musical Variety Hour*, a national weekly radio program broadcast over Station WABC in New York City. During his numerous stage performances Vallee invariably sang through a trademark megaphone. Among his most famous hit numbers were "Deep Heart," "As Time Goes By" and "I'm Just a Vagabond Lover." These well-wishers did not know that the debonair crooner was endeavoring to gain "some breathing space" amidst an acrimonious divorce from his actress wife, Fay Webb.

When the train arrived at 9:20 a.m. most of the crowd had been on the scene for ninety minutes. Among this assemblage were Mayor Lawrence B. Owens and Charles Miot, the township auditorium manager. George "Buck" Buchanan, the Columbia *Record* manager, decided to cover personally this breaking story.

After the locomotive arrived at the station, however, there was no sign of Vallee. As Buchanan later wrote, "When it pulled up and Rudy wasn't on the platform the whole crowd was ready to climb on the train to find him." Eventually a spokesman appeared to announce that the singer was about to come out. He had been eating breakfast when the Orange Blossom Special reached Columbia. The aide also declared that Vallee and his entourage had not anticipated this warm reception. Meanwhile, Mayor Owens had arranged for the train stopover to be extended for twenty minutes.

Within a few minutes Vallee was outside "attired in a blue shirt, minus a necktie, along with a tan flannel suit. He made a great effort to be "very charming" to his numerous fans. He happily shouted out his trademark greeting, "Heigh-Ho Everybody." Vallee told Buchanan that he had been using that phrase since his earliest days at the Heigh-Ho Supper Club in New York City. Throughout this event Vallee's publicity photographer was catching everything on a film camera.

The crooner graciously consented to stroll a couple blocks up Gervais Street with Mayor Owens and several other dignitaries. Although Vallee answered several of Buchanan's questions, he said nothing that was noteworthy. He also was carrying an expensive new Kodak camera, with which he took several pictures of his various walking companions. "No, they are just for my own pleasure," he cheerfully announced. He stressed to Mayor Owens, "If I ever should happen to get anything…like an airplane crash they [a newspaper] could use it."

Not surprisingly, various members of the Connecticut Yankee Orchestra mingled with the crowd on the platform. Interestingly, several other celebrities may have circulated about without attracting any notice. Buchanan later heard that the Hollywood film actress Anne Harding also was on that train. But she definitely was not traveling with Vallee's party. Sports enthusiasts were dismayed to learn belatedly that several New York Yankee ballplayers, including Bill Dickey and Lefty Gomez, were passengers as well. They were en route to the Yankees' spring training camp at St. Petersburg, Florida.

Upon making a few parting comments, Vallee boarded the Orange Blossom Special. He professed to be looking forward to his upcoming engagement at the Township Auditorium. All told, everyone thoroughly enjoyed their initial encounter with the famous crooner. Hopefully, Rudy Vallee's subsequent singing performance was equally as satisfying.

About the Author

A native of Pennsylvania, Dr. Miles S. Richards has resided in Columbia since 1983. He has gained advanced history degrees, notably a doctorate from the University of South Carolina, and he currently serves on the history faculty at Midlands Technical College in Columbia. He has written numerous works in scholarly history journals and other publications. He also is active within historical organizations in South Carolina.